W9-AZZ-530

GACE
026
027

Biology
Teacher Certification Exam

By: Sharon Wynne, M.S.
Southern Connecticut State University

"And, while there's no reason yet to panic, I think it's only prudent that we make preparations to panic."

MANKOFF

XAMonline, INC.
Boston

To obtain permission(s) to use the material from this work for any purpose including workshops or seminars, please submit a written request to:

XAMonline, Inc.
21 Orient Ave.
Melrose, MA 02176
Toll Free 1-800-509-4128
Email: info@xamonline.com
Web www.xamonline.com
Fax: 1-781-662-9268

Library of Congress Cataloging-in-Publication Data

Wynne, Sharon A.
    GACE Biology 026/027: Teacher Certification / Sharon A. Wynne. -2nd ed.
    ISBN 978-1-58197-528-4
    1. GACE Biology 026/027.   2. Study Guides.   3. GACE
    4. Teachers' Certification & Licensure.   5. Careers

Disclaimer:

The material presented in this publication is the sole work of XAMonline and was created independently from the National Education Association, Educational Testing Service, or any State Department of Education, National Evaluation Systems or other testing affiliates.

Between the time of publication and printing, state specific standards, testing formats, and website information may change. XAMonline developed the sample test questions and they reflect similar content as on real tests; however, they are not former tests. XAMonline assembles content that aligns with state standards, but makes no claims nor guarantees regarding test performance. Numerical scores are determined by testing companies such as NES or ETS and then are compared with individual state standards. A passing score varies from state to state.

Printed in the United States of America   œ-1

GACE: Biology 026, 027
ISBN: 978-1-58197-7738

Table of Contents

Great Study and Testing Tips!

What to study in order to prepare for the subject assessments is the focus of this study guide, but equally important is *how* you study.

You can increase your chances of truly mastering the information by taking some simple, but effective steps.

Study Tips:

1. Some foods aid the learning process. Foods such as milk, nuts, seeds, rice, and oats help your study efforts by releasing natural memory enhancers called CCKs (*cholecystokinins*) composed of *tryptopha*n, *choline*, and *phenylalanine*. All of these chemicals enhance the neurotransmitters associated with memory. Before studying, try a light, protein-rich meal of eggs, turkey, and fish. All of these foods release the memory enhancing chemicals. The better the connections, the more you comprehend.

Likewise, before you take a test, stick to a light snack of energy boosting and relaxing foods. A glass of milk, a piece of fruit, or some peanuts all release various memory-boosting chemicals and help you relax and focus on the subject at hand.

2. Learn to take great notes. A by-product of our modern culture is that we have grown accustomed to getting our information in short doses (e.g., TV news sound bites or USA Today style newspaper articles). Consequently, we've subconsciously trained ourselves to assimilate information better in neat little packages. If your notes are scrawled all over the paper, it fragments the flow of the information. Strive for clarity. Newspapers use a standard format to achieve clarity. Your notes can be much clearer through use of proper formatting. A very effective format is called the *"Cornell Method."*

Take a sheet of loose-leaf lined notebook paper and draw a line all the way down the paper about 1-2" from the left-hand edge.

Draw another line across the width of the paper about 1-2" up from the bottom. Repeat this process on the reverse side of the page.

Look at the highly effective result. You have ample room for notes, a left hand margin for special emphasis items or inserting supplementary data from the textbook, a large area at the bottom for a brief summary, and a little rectangular space for just about anything you want.

3. Get the concept then the details. Too often we focus on the details and fail to gather an understanding of the concept. If you simply memorize dates, places, and names, you may well miss the whole point of the subject.

Putting concepts in your own words can increase your understanding. If you are working from a textbook, automatically summarize each paragraph in your mind. If you are outlining text, don't simply copy the author's words, *rephrase* them in your own words.

You remember your own thoughts and words much better than someone else's, and subconsciously tend to associate the important details to the core concepts.

4. Ask Why? Pull apart written material paragraph by paragraph and don't forget the captions under the illustrations.

Example: If the heading is "Stream Erosion", flip it around to read "Why do streams erode?" Then answer the question.

If you train your mind to think in a series of questions and answers, not only will you learn more, but you will decrease your test anxiety by increasing your familiarity with the question and answer process.

5. Read for reinforcement and future needs. Even if you only have ten minutes, put your notes or a book in your hand. Your mind is similar to a computer, you have to input data in order to process it. *By reading, you are creating the neural connections for future retrieval.* The more times you read something, the more you reinforce the learning of ideas.

Even if you don't fully understand something on the first pass, *your mind stores much of the material for later recall.*

6. Relax to learn so go into exile. Our bodies respond to an inner clock in cycles called biorhythms. Burning the midnight oil works well for some people, but not everyone.

If possible, set aside a particular place to study that is free of distractions. Shut off the television, cell phone, and pager and exile your friends and family during your study period.

If silence really bothers you, try background music. Light classical music at a low volume has been shown to aid in concentration. Music that evokes pleasant emotions without lyrics is highly suggested. Try just about anything by Mozart. It relaxes you.

7. <u>**Use arrows not highlighters.**</u> At best, it's difficult to read a page full of yellow, pink, blue, and green streaks. Try staring at a neon sign for a while and you'll soon see that the horde of colors obscures the message.

A quick note, a brief dash of color, an underline, and an arrow pointing to a particular passage is much clearer than a horde of highlighted words.

8. <u>**Budget your study time.**</u> Although you shouldn't ignore any of the material, *allocate your available study time in the same ratio that topics may appear on the test.*

Testing Tips:

1. <u>Get smart, play dumb</u>. Don't read anything into the question. Don't make an assumption that the test writer is looking for something else than what is asked.

2. <u>Read the question and all the choices *twice* before answering the question</u>. You may miss something by not carefully reading and re-reading both the question and the answers.

If you really don't have a clue as to the right answer, leave it blank on the first time through. Go on to the other questions, as they may provide a clue as to how to answer the skipped questions.

If later on, you still can't answer the questions you've skipped . . . **Guess.** The only penalty for guessing is that you *might* get it wrong. Only one thing is certain; if you don't put anything down, you will get it wrong!

3. <u>Turn the question into a statement</u>. Look at the wording of the questions. The syntax of the question usually provides a clue. Does it seem more familiar as a statement rather than as a question? Does it sound strange?

By turning a question into a statement, you may be able to spot if an answer sounds right, and it may also trigger memories of material you have read.

4. <u>Look for hidden clues</u>. It's actually very difficult to compose multiple-foil (choice) questions without giving away part of the answer in the options presented.

In most multiple-choice questions you can often readily eliminate one or two of the potential answers. This leaves you with only two real possibilities and automatically your odds go to fifty-fifty with very little work.

5. <u>Trust your instincts</u>. On questions that you aren't really certain about, go with your basic instincts. **Your first impression on how to answer a question is usually correct.**

6. <u>Mark your answers directly on the test booklet</u>. Don't bother trying to fill in the optical scan sheet on the first pass through the test.

Just be very careful not to miss-mark your answers when you eventually transcribe them to the scan sheet.

7. <u>Watch the clock!</u> You have a set amount of time to answer the questions. Don't get bogged down trying to answer a single question at the expense of ten questions you can more readily answer.

COMPETENCY 1.0   **UNDERSTAND CELL STRUCTURE AND FUNCTION**

Skill 1.1 Demonstrating knowledge of the components of cells (e.g., cell membrane, cell wall, ribosome, nucleus, mitochondrion, chloroplast) and how the structure of cell organelles relates to their function

The cell is the basic unit of all living things. There are three types of cells: prokaryotic, eukaryotic, and archaea. Archaea have some similarities with prokaryotes, but are as distantly related to prokaryotes as prokaryotes are to eukaryotes.

PROKARYOTES

Prokaryotes consist only of bacteria and cyanobacteria (formerly known as blue-green algae). The diagram below shows the classification of prokaryotes.

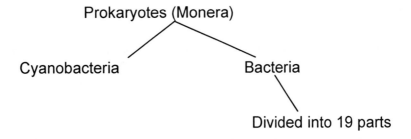

Bacterial cells have no defined nucleus or nuclear membrane. The DNA, RNA, and ribosomes float freely within the cell. The cytoplasm has a single chromosome condensed to form a **nucleoid**. Prokaryotes have a thick cell wall made up of amino sugars (glycoproteins) that provides protection, gives the cell shape, and keeps the cell from bursting. The antibiotic penicillin targets the **cell wall** of bacteria. Penicillin works by disrupting the cell wall, thus killing the cell.

The cell wall surrounds the **plasma membrane** (cell membrane). The plasma membrane consists of a lipid bilayer that controls the passage of molecules in and out of the cell. Some prokaryotes have a capsule made of polysaccharides that surrounds the cell wall for extra protection from other organisms or the environment.

Many bacterial cells have appendages used for movement called **flagella**. Some cells also have **pili**, which are a protein strand used for attachment. Pili may also be used for sexual conjugation (where bacterial cells exchange DNA).

BIOLOGY   1

Prokaryotes are the most numerous and widespread organisms on earth. Bacteria were most likely the first cells and evidenece of them dates back in the fossil record to 3.5 billion years ago. Their ability to adapt to the environment allows them to thrive in a wide variety of habitats.

EUKARYOTES

Eukaryotic cells are found in protists, fungi, plants, and animals. Most eukaryotic cells are larger than prokaryotic cells. They contain many organelles, which are membrane-bound areas used for specific functions. Their cytoplasm contains a cytoskeleton which provides a protein framework for the cell. The cytoplasm also supports the organelles and contains the ions and molecules necessary for cell function. The cytoplasm is contained by the plasma membrane. The plasma membrane allows molecules to pass in and out of the cell. The membrane can bud inward to engulf outside material in a process called endocytosis. Exocytosis is a secretory mechanism, the reverse of endocytosis.

ARCHAEA

There are three kinds of organisms with archaea cells: **methanogens**, obligate anaerobes that produce methane, **halobacteria**, which can live only in concentrated brine solutions, and **thermoacidophiles**, which can live only in acidic hot springs.

Compare and contrast archaea, prokaryotes, and eukaryotes

The most significant difference between prokaryotes and eukaryotes is that eukaryotes have a **nucleus**. The nucleus is the "brain" of the cell that contains all of the cell's genetic information. The chromosomes consist of chromatin, which are complexes of DNA and proteins. The chromosomes are tightly coiled to conserve space while providing a large surface area. The nucleus is the site of transcription of the DNA into RNA. The **nucleolus** is where ribosomes are made. There is at least one of these dark-staining bodies inside the nucleus of most eukaryotes. The nuclear envelope consists of two membranes separated by a narrow space. The envelope contains many pores that let RNA out of the nucleus.

Ribosomes are the site for protein synthesis. Ribosomes may be free floating in the cytoplasm or attached to the endoplasmic reticulum. There may be up to a half a million ribosomes in a cell, depending on how much protein the cell makes. Ribosomes are found in both prokaryotic and eukaryotic cells.

The **endoplasmic reticulum** (ER) is folded and has a large surface area. It is the "roadway" of the cell and allows for transport of materials through and out of the cell. There are two types of ER: smooth and rough. Smooth endoplasmic reticula contain no ribosomes on their surface and are the site of lipid synthesis. Rough endoplasmic reticula have ribosomes on their surface and aid in the synthesis of proteins that are membrane bound or destined for secretion. The endoplasmic reticulum is found only in eukaryotic cells.

Many of the products made in the ER proceed to the Golgi apparatus. The **Golgi apparatus** functions to sort, modify, and package molecules that are made in the other parts of the cell (like the ER). These molecules are either sent out of the cell or to other organelles within the cell. The Golgi apparatus is found only in eukaryotic cells.

Lysosomes are found mainly in animal cells. These contain digestive enzymes that break down food, unnecessary substances, viruses, damaged cell components, and, eventually, the cell itself. It is believed that lysosomes play a role in the aging process. Lysosomes are found only in eukaryotic cells.

Mitochondria are large organelles that are the site of cellular respiration, the production of ATP that supplies energy to the cell. Muscle cells have many mitochondria because they use a great deal of energy. Mitochondria have their own DNA, RNA, and ribosomes and are capable of reproducing by binary fission if there is a great demand for additional energy. Mitochondria have two membranes: a smooth outer membrane and a folded inner membrane. The folds inside the mitochondria are called cristae. They provide a large surface area for cellular respiration to occur. The space inside the innermost membrane is called the matrix. Mitochondria are found only in eukaryotic cells.

Plastids are found only in photosynthetic organisms. They are similar to the mitochondira due to the double membrane structure. They also have their own DNA, RNA, and ribosomes and can reproduce if the need for the increased capture of sunlight becomes necessary. There are several types of plastids. **Chloroplasts** are the site of photosynthesis. The stroma is the thick fluid inside the chloroplast's inner membrane space. The stoma encloses sacs called thylakoids that contain the photosynthetic pigment chlorophyll. The chlorophyll traps sunlight inside the thylakoid to generate ATP which is used in the stroma to produce carbohydrates and other products. The **chromoplasts** make and store yellow and orange pigments. They provide color to leaves, flowers, and fruits. The **amyloplasts** store starch and are used as a food reserve. They are abundant in roots like potatoes. Plastids are found only in eukaryotic cells.

The Endosymbiotic Theory states that mitochondria and chloroplasts were once free living and possibly evolved from prokaryotic cells. At some point in eukaryotic evolutionary history, they entered the eukaryotic cell and maintained a symbiotic relationship with the cell, with both the cell and organelle benefiting from the relationship. The fact that they both have their own DNA, RNA, ribosomes, and are capable of reproduction supports this theory.

Found only in plant cells or prokaryotic cells, the **cell wall** is composed of cellulose and fibers. It is thick enough for support and protection, yet porous enough to allow water and dissolved substances to enter. **Vacuoles** are found mostly in plant cells. They hold stored food and pigments. Their large size allows them to fill with water in order to provide turgor pressure. Lack of turgor pressure causes a plant to wilt. Vacuoles are found only in eukaryotic cells.

The **cytoskeleton**, found in both animal and plant cells, is composed of protein filaments attached to the plasma membrane and organelles. The cytoskeleton provides a framework for the cell and aids in cell movement. Three types of fibers make up the cytoskeleton:

1.   **Microtubules** – The largest of the three fibers, they make up cilia and eukaryotic flagella for locomotion. Some examples are sperm cells, cilia that line the fallopian tubes, and tracheal cilia. Centrioles are also composed of microtubules. They aid in cell division to form the spindle fibers that pull the cell apart into two new cells. Centrioles are not found in the cells of higher plants.

2.   **Intermediate filaments** – Intermediate in size, they are smaller than microtubules, but larger than microfilaments. They help the cell keep its shape.

3.   **Microfilaments** – Smallest of the three fibers, they are made of actin and small amounts of myosin. They function in cell movement like cytoplasmic streaming, endocytosis, and ameboid movement. Microfilaments are used to pinch the cell into two parts after cell division, forming two new cells by a process known as cytokinesis.

The following is a diagram of a generalized animal cell.

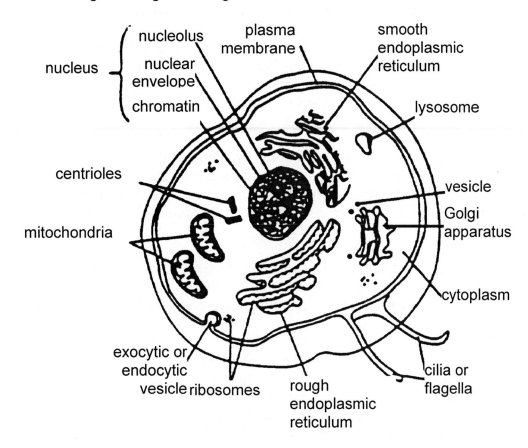

Skill 1.2 Comparing the characteristics of prokaryotic and eukaryotic cells

See Skill 1.1

Skill 1.3 Analyzing the interactions among cell organelles (e.g., phagocytosis)

The transport of large molecules depends on the fluidity of the membrane, which is controlled by cholesterol in the membrane. **Exocytosis** is the release of large particles by vesicles fusing with the plasma membrane. In the process of **endocytosis**, the cell takes in macromolecules and particulate matter by forming vesicles derived from the plasma membrane. There are three types of endocytosis in animal cells. **Phagocytosis** is when a particle is engulfed by pseudopodia and packaged in a vacuole. In **pinocytosis**, the cell takes in extracellular fluid in small vesicles. **Receptor-mediated endocytosis** is when the membrane vesicles bud inward to allow a cell to take in large amounts of certain substances. The vesicles have proteins with receptors that are specific for the substance.

Skill 1.4 Demonstrating knowledge of the structure and function of different types of cell (e.g., muscle cells, nerve cells, guard cells)

The function of different systems in organisms from bacteria to humans dictates system structure. The basic principle that "form follows function" applies to all organismal systems. We will discuss a few examples to illustrate this principle. Keep in mind that we can relate the structure and function of all organismal systems.

Mitochondria, subcellular organelles present in eukaryotic cells, provide energy for cell functions. Much of the energy-generating activity takes place in the mitochondrial inner membrane. To maximize this activity, the mitochondrial membrane has many folds to pack a relatively large amount of membrane into a small space.

Bacterial cells maintain a high surface area to volume ratio to maximize contact with the environment and allow for exchange of nutrients and waste products. Bacterial cells achieve this high ratio by maintaining a small internal volume by cell division.

The cardiovascular system of animals has many specialized structures that help achieve the function of delivering blood to all parts of the body. The heart has four chambers for the delivery and reception of blood. The blood vessels vary in size to accommodate the necessary volume of blood. For example, vessels near the heart are large to accommodate large amounts of blood and vessels in the extremities are very small to limit the amount of blood delivered.

Animals use muscles to convert the chemical energy of ATP into mechanical work. A muscle is composed of bundles of specialized cells capable of creating movement through a combination of contraction and relaxation. Muscle fibers are grouped according to where they are found (skeletal muscle, smooth muscle, and cardiac muscle). A skeletal muscle fiber is not a single cell, but is commonly thought of as the unit of a muscle and is composed of myofibrils. Smooth muscle, including the human heart, is composed of individual cells each containing thick (myosin) and thin (actin) filaments that slide against each other to produce contraction of the cell.

All cells exhibit a voltage difference across the cell membrane. In animals, nerve cells and muscle cells are excitable. Their cell membrane can produce electrochemical impulses and conduct them along the membrane. The nerve cell may be divided into three main parts: the cell body or soma, short processes called the dendrites, and a single long nerve fiber, the axon. The body of a nerve cell is similar to that of other cells in that it includes the nucleus, mitochondria, endoplasmic reticulum, ribosomes, and other organelles. The dendrites receive impulses from other cells and transfer them to the cell body. The effect of these impulses may be excitatory or inhibitory. The long nerve fiber, the axon, transfers the signal from the cell body to other nerve or muscle cells.

In plants, guard cells control the stomata (openings for gas exchange) found in the epidermis of the leaf. These plant cells are regulated by the environmental factors of light intensity, CO_2 concentration and water availability. When the guard cells are activated, potassium pumps actively transport K^+ (potassium) into the guard cells, resulting in a high concentration of K^+ inside the cells. As a result, water enters the cells by osmosis. This causes the guard cells to swell. When the stoma is open CO_2 can diffuse into the leaf and enter the Calvin Cycle. The oxygen produced in photosynthesis diffuses out of the open stoma. Water vapor also escapes from the stoma by the process of transpiration.

Finally, the structure of the skeletal systems of different animals varies based on the animal's method of movement. For example, the honeycombed structure of bird bones provides a lightweight skeleton of great strength to accommodate flight. The bones of the human skeletal system are dense, strong, and aligned in such a way as to allow walking on two legs in an upright position.

COMPETENCY 2.0   UNDERSTAND THE BASIC CHEMICAL COMPONENTS AND REACTIONS OF CELLS

Skill 2.1 Recognizing the chemical elements (e.g., carbon, hydrogen, oxygen) necessary for life and demonstrating knowledge of how these elements combine to form biologically important organic and inorganic compounds

All molecules important to life ultimately derive from relatively simple elements and compounds. Once living organisms assimilate these elements and compounds, they form the building blocks of complex compounds. Later, the same organisms break down many of these complex compounds into simple elemental forms. This cycle involves the elements of carbon, oxygen, hydrogen, nitrogen, and a great variety of minerals including phosphorus and sulfur.

The carbon atom can enter into thousands of different combinations within one organism and within thousands of others as the materials are passed on to other organisms. Because carbon has the ability to form four simultaneous covalent bonds, it can form long chains or branched chains and it can bond to many types of atoms. The study of compounds containing carbon is called organic chemistry since carbon compounds are the distinctive component of all living things (animal or plant).

All forms of life require oxygen and hydrogen for a variety of processes. Water, two hydrogen atoms and one oxygen atom, is critical to life. The major inorganic source of oxygen in organic compounds is carbon dioxide (CO_2). Atmospheric oxygen, O_2, is 20% of the atmosphere and is necessary for aerobic metabolism.

Following carbon, hydrogen, and oxygen, the most common element in the materials of life is nitrogen, which is a constituent of all proteins. No animal and only a few plants can utilize nitrogen directly from the atmosphere; however, plants can utilize ammonia (NH_3), nitrates (NO_3), or various nitrites (NO_2) in making proteins. Animals then eat the plants and utilize the plant proteins.

Most living cells also need macronutrients, which include calcium, phosphorus, chlorine, sulfur, potassium, sodium, magnesium, iodine, and iron. Phosphorus is obtained through digestion of phosphates (PO_4) and sulfur is obtained through digestion of sulfates (SO_4), which often are found in combination with various metal elements such as magnesium or iron.

Water is necessary for life. The unique properties of water are due to its molecular structure. Water is an important solvent in biological compounds. Water is a polar substance. This means it is formed by covalent bonds that make it electrically lopsided.

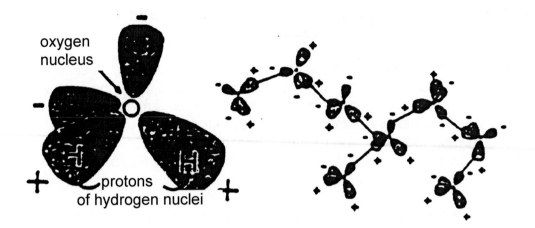

A water molecule showing polarity created by covalent bonds.

Hydrogen bonding between water molecules.

Water molecules are attracted to other water molecules due to electrical attraction and this explains two important properties: adhesion and cohesion.

Adhesion is when water sticks to other substances like the xylem of a stem, which aids the water in traveling up the stem to the leaves.

Cohesion is the ability of water molecules to stick to each other by hydrogen bonding. This allows for surface tension on a body of water, or capillarity, which allows water to move through vessels. Surface tension is how difficult it is to stretch or break the surface of a liquid. Cohesion allows water to move against gravity.

There are several other important properties of water. Water is a good solvent. An aqueous solution is one in which water is the solvent. Water provides a medium in which chemical reactions can occur. Water has a high specific heat of 1 calorie per gram per degree Celsius, allowing it to cool and warm slowly, allowing organisms to adapt to temperature changes. Water has a high boiling point; thus, it is a good coolant. Its ability to evaporate stabilizes the environment and allows organisms to maintain body temperature. Water has a high freezing point and a lower density as a solid than as a liquid. Water is most dense at four degrees Celsius. This allows ice to float on top of water so a whole body of water does not freeze during the winter. Because of this property of water, aquatic animals can survive the winter.

Skill 2.2 Analyzing the differences between anaerobic and aerobic respiration and their products

Cellular respiration is the metabolic pathway in which food (e.g. glucose) is broken down to produce energy in the form of ATP. Both plants and animals utilize respiration to create energy for metabolism. In respiration, energy is released by the transfer of electrons in a process know as an **oxidation-reduction (redox)** reaction. The oxidation phase of this reaction is the loss of an electron and the reduction phase is the gain of an electron. Redox reactions are important for all stages of respiration.

Glycolysis is the first process in respiration. It occurs in the cytoplasm of the cell and does not require oxygen. Each of the ten stages of glycolysis is catalyzed by a specific enzyme. The following is a summary of these stages.

In the first stage the reactant is glucose. For energy to be released from glucose, it must be converted to a reactive compound. This conversion occurs through the phosphorylation of a molecule of glucose by the use of two molecules of ATP. This is an investment of energy by the cell. The 6-carbon product, called fructose -1, 6- bisphosphate, breaks into two 3-carbon molecules of sugar. A phosphate group is added to each sugar molecule and hydrogen atoms are removed. Hydrogen is picked up by NAD^+ (a vitamin). Since there are two sugar molecules, two molecules of NADH are formed. The reduction (addition of hydrogen) of NAD allows the potential for energy transfer during a later process.

As the phosphate bonds are broken, ATP is produced. Two ATP molecules are generated as each original 3-carbon sugar molecule is converted to pyruvic acid (pyruvate). A total of four ATP molecules are made in the four stages. Since two molecules of ATP were needed to start the reaction in stage 1, there is a net gain of two ATP molecules at the end of glycolysis. This accounts for only about two percent of the total energy in a molecule of glucose.

Beginning with pyruvate, which was the end product of glycolysis, the following steps occur before entering the **Krebs cycle**.

1. Pyruvic acid is changed to acetyl-CoA (coenzyme A). This involves a 3-carbon pyruvic acid molecule losing one molecule of carbon dioxide (CO_2) to become a 2-carbon acetyl group. In the process, pyruvic acid loses a hydrogen to NAD^+, which is reduced to NADH.
2. Acetyl CoA enters the Krebs cycle. For each molecule of glucose entering glycolysis, two molecules of Acetyl CoA enter the Krebs cycle (one for each molecule of pyruvic acid formed in glycolysis).

The **Krebs cycle** (also known as the citric acid cycle), occurs in four major steps. First, the 2-carbon acetyl CoA combines with a 4-carbon molecule to form a 6-carbon molecule of citric acid. Next, two carbons are lost as carbon dioxide (CO_2) and a 4-carbon molecule is formed to become available to join with CoA to form citric acid again. Since we started with two molecules of CoA, two turns of the Krebs cycle are necessary to process the original molecule of glucose. In the third step, eight hydrogen atoms are released and picked up by FAD and NAD^+ (both molecules are known as electron carriers).

In summary, for each molecule of CoA (remember there were two to start with) you get:

3 molecules of NADH x 2 cycles

1 molecule of $FADH_2$ x 2 cycles

1 molecule of ATP x 2 cycles

This completes the breakdown of glucose. At this point, a total of four molecules of ATP have been made: two from glycolysis and one from each of the two turns of the Krebs cycle. Six molecules of carbon dioxide have been released, two prior to entering the Krebs cycle and two for each of the two turns of the Krebs cycle. Twelve carrier molecules have been reduced: ten NADH and two $FADH_2$. These carrier molecules will carry electrons to the electron transport chain, described later.

In the Krebs cycle, ATP is made by substrate level phosphorylation. Notice that the Krebs cycle in itself does not produce much ATP, but functions mostly in the reduction of electron carriers which are used in the electron transport chain that makes the most ATP.

In the **Electron Transport Chain,** NADH transfers electrons from glycolysis and the Kreb's cycle to the first molecule in a chain of molecules embedded in the inner membrane of the mitochondrion.

Most of the molecules in the electron transport chain are proteins. Nonprotein molecules are also part of the chain and are essential for the catalytic functions of certain enzymes. The electron transport chain does not make ATP directly. Instead, it breaks up a large free energy drop into a more manageable one. The chain uses electrons to pump H^+ ions across the mitochondrial membrane. The H^+ gradient is used to form ATP synthesis in a process called **chemiosmosis** (oxidative phosphorylation). ATP synthetase and energy generated by the movement of hydrogen ions coming off of NADH and $FADH_2$ builds ATP from ADP on the inner membrane of the mitochondria. Each NADH yields three molecules of ATP (10 x 3) and each $FADH_2$ yields two molecules of ATP (2 x 2). Thus, the electron transport chain and oxidative phosphorylation produces 34 ATP for every molecule of glucose that enters glycolysis.

Thus, the net gain from the whole process of respiration is about 36 molecules of ATP:

> Glycolysis - 4 ATP made, 2 ATP spent = net gain of 2 ATP
> Acetyl CoA- 2 ATP used
> Krebs cycle - 1 ATP made for each turn of the cycle = net gain of 2 ATP
> Electron transport chain - 34 ATP gained

Aerobic versus anaerobic respiration

Cellular respiration generates ATP with oxygen (aerobic) or without oxygen (anaerobic). We have already discussed aerobic respiration. Anaerobic respiration can occur by fermentation. ATP can be generated by fermentation by substrate level phosphorylation if there is enough NAD^+ present to accept electrons during oxidation. In anaerobic respiration, NADH is oxidized by transferring electrons to pyruvate. There are two common types of fermentation.

In **alcoholic fermentation**, pyruvate is converted to ethanol in two steps. In the first step, carbon dioxide is released from the pyruvate. In the second step, ethanol is produced by the reduction of acetaldehyde by NADH. This results in the regeneration of NAD^+ for glycolysis. Alcohol fermentation is carried out by yeast and some bacteria.

Pyruvate is reduced to form lactate as a waste product by NADH in the process of **lactic acid fermentation.** Animal cells and some bacteria that do not use oxygen utilize lactic acid fermentation to make ATP. Lactic acid forms when pyruvic acid accepts hydrogen from NADH. A buildup of lactic acid is what causes muscle soreness following exercise.

Energy remains stored in the lactic acid or alcohol until needed. This is not an efficient type of respiration. When oxygen is present, aerobic respiration occurs after glycolysis.

Both aerobic and anaerobic pathways oxidize glucose to pyruvate by glycolysis and both pathways utilize NAD^+ as the oxidizing agent. A substantial difference between the two pathways is that in fermentation an organic molecule such as pyruvate or acetaldehyde is the final electron acceptor. In respiration, the final electron acceptor is oxygen. Another key difference is that respiration yields much more energy from a sugar molecule than does fermentation. Aerobic respiration can produce up to 18 times more ATP than fermentation.

Skill 2.3 Recognizing the role of enzymes as catalysts in cellular reactions and factors that influence enzyme function

Enzymes act as biological catalysts to speed up reactions. Enzymes are the most diverse of all types of proteins. They are not used up in a reaction and are recyclable. Each enzyme catalyzes a specific reaction. Enzymes act on a substrate. The substrate is the material to be broken down or put together. Most enzymes end in the suffix -ase (lipase, amylase). The prefix usually is the substrate being acted on (lipids, sugars).

$$\text{Substrate} \xrightarrow{\text{Enzyme}} \text{Product}$$

The active site is the region of the enzyme that binds to the substrate. There are two theories for how the active site functions. The **lock and key theory** states that the shape of the enzyme is specific because it fits into the substrate like a key fits into a lock. It aids in holding molecules close together so reactions can easily occur. The **Induced fit theory** states that an enzyme can stretch and bend to fit the substrate. This is the most accepted theory.

Many factors can influence enzyme activity, including temperature and pH. The temperature can impact the rate of reaction of an enzyme. The optimal pH for most enzymes is between 6 and 8, with a few enzymes whose optimal pH falls out of this range.

Cofactors aid in the function of some enzymes. Cofactors may be inorganic or organic. Organic cofactors are known as coenzymes. Vitamins are examples of coenzymes. Some chemicals can inhibit an enzyme's function. **Competitive inhibitors** block the substrate from entering the active site of the enzyme to reduce productivity. **Noncompetitive inhibitors** bind to the enzyme in a location not in the active site but still interrupt substrate binding. In most cases, noncompetitive inhibitors alter the shape of the enzyme. An **allosteric enzyme** can exist in two shapes, they are active in one form and inactive in the other. Overactive enzymes may cause metabolic diseases.

Skill 2.4 Identifying the structure and function of different biomolecules (e.g., carbohydrates, lipids, proteins, nucleic acids)

A compound consists of two or more elements in a fixed ratio. There are four major types of chemical compounds found in the cells and bodies of living things. These are carbohydrates, lipids, proteins, and nucleic acids.

Monomers are the simplest unit of structure. **Monomers** combine to form **polymers**, or long chains, making a large variety of molecules. Monomers combine through the process of condensation reactions (also called dehydration synthesis). In this process, one molecule of water is removed between each of two adjoining monomers. In order to break the polymer apart into monomers, water molecules are added. This process is called hydrolysis.

Carbohydrates contain a ratio of two hydrogen atoms for each carbon and oxygen $(CH_2O)_n$. Carbohydrates include sugars and starches. They function in the release of energy. **Monosaccharides** are the simplest sugars and include glucose, fructose, and galactose. Carbohydrates are major nutrients for cells. In cellular respiration, the cells extract the energy from glucose molecules. **Disaccharides** are made by joining two monosaccharides by condensation to form a glycosidic linkage (covalent bond between two monosaccharides). Maltose is the combination of two glucose molecules, lactose is the combination of glucose and galactose, and sucrose is the combination of glucose and fructose.

Polysaccharides consist of many monomers joined together. They are storage material hydrolyzed as needed to provide sugar for cells or building material for structures protecting the cell. Examples of polysaccharides include starch, glycogen, cellulose, and chitin.

Starch - major energy storage molecule in plants. It is a polymer consisting of glucose monomers.

Glycogen - major energy storage molecule in animals. It is made up of many glucose monomers.

Cellulose - found in plant cell walls, its function is structural. Most animals lack the enzymes necessary to hydrolyze cellulose, so it simply adds bulk (fiber) to the diet.

Chitin - found in the exoskeleton of arthropods and fungi. Chitin contains an amino sugar (glycoprotein).

Lipids are composed of glycerol (an alcohol) bonded to fatty acid tails. Lipids are **hydrophobic** (water fearing) and will not mix with water. There are three important families of lipids: fats, phospholipids, and steroids.

Fats consist of glycerol (alcohol) and three fatty acids. Fatty acids are long carbon skeletons. The nonpolar carbon-hydrogen bonds in the tails of fatty acids are highly hydrophobic. Fats are solids at room temperature and come from animal sources (e.g., butter and lard); oils are liquid at room temperature and come from animal or plant sources.

Phospholipids are a vital component in cell membranes. In a phospholipid, one or two fatty acids are replaced by a phosphate group linked to a nitrogen group. They consist of a **polar** (charged) head that is hydrophilic (water loving) and a **nonpolar** (uncharged) tail which is hydrophobic. Plasma membranes are composed of a phospholipid bilayer such that the phosopholipids in the membrane can orient with the polar heads facing the interstitial fluid found outside the cell and also facing the internal fluid of the cell while the nonpolar tails face each other in the interior of the membrane itself.

Steroids are insoluble in water and are composed of a carbon skeleton consisting of four inter-connected rings. An important steroid is cholesterol, which is the precursor for other steroids. Hormones, including cortisone, testosterone, estrogen, and progesterone, are steroids. Their insolubility keeps them from dissolving in body fluids.

Proteins compose about fifty percent of the dry weight of animals and bacteria. Proteins function in structure and support (e.g., connective tissue, hair, feathers, and quills), storage of amino acids (e.g., albumin in eggs and casein in milk), transport of substances (e.g. hemoglobin), coordination body activities (e.g. insulin), signal transduction (e.g. membrane receptor proteins), contraction (e.g., muscles, cilia, and flagella), body defense (e.g. antibodies), and as enzymes to speed up chemical reactions.

All proteins are polymers made of monomers known as **amino acids**. There are twenty distinct amino acids. An amino acid contains an amino group, an acid group, and a radical—or "r"—group. The radical group varies and defines the amino acid. Amino acids monomers are joined into protein polymers through condensation reactions. The covalent bond formed between two amino acids is called a peptide bond. Polymers of amino acids are called polypeptide chains. An analogy can be drawn between the twenty amino acids and the alphabet. We can form millions of words using an alphabet of only twenty-six letters. Similarly, organisms can create many different proteins using only twenty amino acids. This results in the formation of many different proteins, where structure defines function.

There are four levels of protein structure: primary, secondary, tertiary, and quaternary.

Primary structure is the protein's unique sequence of amino acids. A slight change in primary structure can alter a protein's conformation, or shape, and its ability to function. **Secondary structure** describes the coils and folds of polypeptide chains. The coils and folds are the result of hydrogen bonds along the polypeptide backbone. The secondary structure is either in the form of an "alpha helix" or a "pleated sheet." The alpha helix is a coil held together by hydrogen bonds. A pleated sheet is the polypeptide chain folding back and forth. The hydrogen bonds between parallel regions hold it together. **Tertiary structure** is formed by bonding between the side chains of the amino acids. For example, disulfide bridges form when two sulfhydryl groups on the amino acids bond together to form a strong covalent bond. **Quaternary structure** is the overall structure of the protein from the aggregation of two or more polypeptide chains. An example of quaternary structure can be found in hemoglobin, which consists of two kinds of polypeptide chains.

Nucleic acids consist of DNA (deoxyribonucleic acid) and RNA (ribonucleic acid).

Nucleic acids contain the code for the amino acid sequence of proteins and the instructions for self-replicating. The monomer of nucleic acids is called a nucleotide. A nucleotide consists of a 5-carbon sugar (deoxyribose in DNA, ribose in RNA), a phosphate group, and a nitrogenous base. The base sequence contains the molecular code, or "instructions." There are five bases: adenine, thymine, cytosine, guanine, and uracil. Uracil is found only in RNA and replaces thymine, found only in DNA. The following provides a summary of nucleic acid structure:

	SUGAR	PHOSPHATE	BASES
DNA	deoxy-ribose	present	adenine, thymine, cytosine, guanine
RNA	ribose	present	adenine, uracil, cytosine, guanine

Due to molecular structure, adenine always pairs with thymine in DNA or uracil in RNA. Cytosine always pairs with guanine in both DNA and RNA.

This allows for the symmetry of the DNA molecule seen below.

RNA
(single-stranded)

DNA
(double-stranded)

In DNA, adenine and thymine are linked by two covalent bonds and cytosine and guanine are linked by three covalent bonds. Guanine and cytosine are harder to break apart than thymine (uracil) and adenine because of the greater number of bonds between the bases. The double-stranded DNA molecule forms a double helix, or twisted ladder, shape.

COMPETENCY 3.0 UNDERSTAND THE PHYSIOLOGICAL PROCESSES OF CELLS

Skill 3.1 Demonstrating knowledge of how cells maintain homeostasis (e.g., the effect of concentration gradients, rate of movement, and surface area/volume ratio)

All living organisms respond to and adapt to their environments. Homeostasis is the result of regulatory mechanisms that help maintain an organism's internal environment within tolerable limits. It is important to recognize that homeostasis is not a single process. Instead, homeostasis is the combined result of many small changes throughout multiple parts of an organism. These small changes and cycles result in the overall state of constancy, which ensures survival.

Cell membranes are selectively permeable, which is the key to transport. Not all molecules may pass through easily. In humans and mammals, the skeletal system acts as a buffer in maintaining calcium homeostasis by absorbing or releasing calcium as needed. The muscular system contributes to homeostasis in two ways. First, muscle contraction produces heat as a by-product. This heat helps maintain the body's internal temperature. Second, the muscular system (in coordination with the skeletal system) allows organisms to move to environments that are more favorable from a homeostatic perspective.

The circulatory system also plays a vital role in homeostasis. The circulatory system delivers nutrients and removes waste from all the body's tissue by pumping blood through blood vessels. Constriction and dilation of blood vessels near the skin help maintain body temperature. The entire function of the immune system is homeostatic in nature. The immune system protects the body's internal environment from invading microorganisms, viruses, and cancerous cells.

There are three homeostatic systems to regulate differences in concentration, waste removal, and temperature. **Osmoregulation** deals with maintenance of the appropriate level of water and salts in body fluids for optimum cellular functions. **Excretion** is the elimination of metabolic waste products from the body including excess water. **Thermoregulation** maintains the internal, or core, body temperature of the organism within a tolerable range for metabolic and cellular processes.

Skill 3.2 Analyzing the processes of photosynthesis and cellular respiration and the relationships between the two processes

See also Skill 2.2 (cellular respiration)

Photosynthesis is an anabolic process that stores energy in the form of a three carbon sugar.

Photosynthesis occurs in organisms that contain chloroplasts, such as plants and some protists, and in certain bacteria. There are a few terms to be familiar with when discussing photosynthesis.

An **autotroph** (self-eater) is an organism that makes its own food from the energy of the sun or other elements. Autotrophs include:

1. **photoautotrophs** – make energy molecules from light and carbon dioxide. Plants, some protists, and some bacteria are photoautotrophs.
2. **chemoautotrophs** – make energy molecules by oxidizing sulfur and ammonia. Some bacteria are chemoautotrophs.

Heterotrophs (other eater) are organisms that must eat other living things to obtain energy. Another term for heterotroph is **consumer**. All animals are heterotrophs. **Decomposers** break down once-living things. Some bacteria and fungi are examples of decomposers. **Scavengers** eat dead things. Examples of scavengers are some bacteria and some animals.

The **chloroplast** is the site of plant and protist photosynthesis. It is similar to the mitochondria due to the increased surface area of the thylakoid membrane. It also contains a fluid called stroma between the stacks of thylakoids. The thylakoid membrane contains pigments (chlorophyll) that are capable of capturing light energy.

Photosynthesis reverses the electron flow found in cellular respiration. Water is split by the chloroplast into hydrogen and oxygen. The oxygen is given off as a waste product as carbon dioxide is reduced to sugar (glucose). This requires the input of energy, which comes from the sun.

Photosynthesis occurs in two stages, the light reactions and the Calvin cycle (dark reactions). The conversion of solar energy to chemical energy occurs in the light reactions. Electrons are transferred by the absorption of light by chlorophyll and cause water to split, releasing oxygen as a waste product. The chemical energy created in the light reaction is in the form of NADPH. ATP is also produced by a process called photophosphorylation. These forms of energy are produced in the thylakoids and are used in the Calvin cycle to produce sugar.

The second stage of photosynthesis is the **Calvin cycle**. Carbon dioxide in the air is incorporated into organic molecules already in the chloroplast. The NADPH produced in the light reaction is used to reduce carbohydrates. ATP from the light reaction is also needed to drive the Calvin cycle.

The process of photosynthesis is made possible by the presence of the sun. Visible light ranges in wavelengths of 750 nanometers (red light) to 380 nanometers (violet light). As wavelength decreases, the amount of energy available increases. Light is carried as photons, which are fixed quantities of energy. Light is reflected (what we see), transmitted, or absorbed (what the plant uses). The plant's pigments capture light of specific wavelengths. Remember that the light that is reflected is what we see as color. Plant pigments include:

Chlorophyll *a* - reflects green/blue light; absorbs red light
Chlorophyll *b* - reflects yellow/green light; absorbs red light
Carotenoids - reflects yellow/orange; absorbs violet/blue light

The pigments absorb photons. The energy from the light excites electrons in the chlorophyll that jump to orbitals with more potential energy and reach an "excited" or unstable state.

These high energy electrons are trapped by primary electron acceptors which are located on the thylakoid membrane. These electron acceptors and the pigments form reaction centers called photosystems that are capable of capturing light energy. Photosystems contain a reaction-center chlorophyll that releases an electron to the primary electron acceptor. This transfer is the first step of the light reactions. There are two photosystems, named according to their date of discovery, not their order of occurrence.

Photosystem I is composed of a pair of chlorophyll *a* molecules. Photosystem I is also called P700 because it absorbs light of 700 nanometers. Photosystem I makes ATP whose energy is needed to build glucose.

Photosystem II is also called P680 because it absorbs light of 680 nanometers. Photosystem II produces ATP + $NADPH_2$ and the waste gas oxygen.

Both photosystems are bound to the **thylakoid membrane**, close to the electron acceptors.

The production of ATP is termed **photophosphorylation** due to the use of light. Photosystem I can use cyclic photophosphorylation where the electron's path occurs in a cycle. It can also use noncyclic photophosphorylation which starts with light and ends with glucose. Photosystem II uses noncyclic photophosphorylation only.

The chemical formula for photosynthesis is:

$$6CO_2 + 12H_2O + \text{energy (from sunlight)} \rightarrow C_6H_{12}O_6 + 6O_2 + 6H_2O$$

Below is a diagram of the relationship between cellular respiration and photosynthesis.

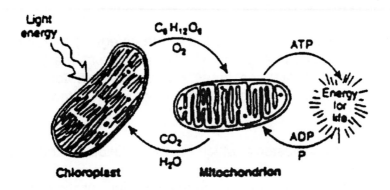

Skill 3.3 Analyzing trans-membrane transport mechanisms (e.g., active and passive transport, facilitated diffusion)

In order to understand cellular transport, it is important to understand the structure of the cell membrane. All organisms contain cell membranes because they regulate the flow of materials into and out of the cell. The current model for the cell membrane is the Fluid Mosaic Model, which takes into account the ability of lipids and proteins to move and change places, giving the membrane fluidity.

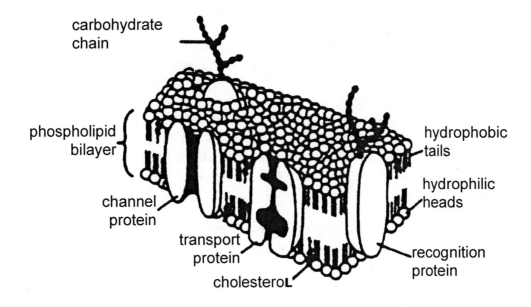

Cell membranes have the following characteristics:

1. They are largely composed of phospholipids which have one polar, charged head with a phosphate group that is hydrophilic (water loving) and two nonpolar lipid tails which are hydrophobic (water fearing). This allows the membrane to orient itself with the polar heads facing the fluid inside and outside the cell and with the hydrophobic lipid tails sandwiched in between.

2. They contain proteins embedded inside (integral proteins) and proteins on the surface (peripheral proteins). These proteins may act as channels for transport, may contain enzymes, may act as receptor sites, may act to stick cells together, or may attach to the cytoskeleton to give the cell shape.

3. They contain cholesterol, which alters the fluidity of the membrane.

4. They usually contain oligosaccharides (small carbohydrate polymers) on the outside of the membrane. These act as markers that help distinguish one cell from another.

5. They usually contain receptors made of glycoproteins that can attach to certain molecules, like hormones.

Cell transport is necessary to maintain homeostasis, or balance between the cell and its external environment. Cell membranes are selectively permeable, which is the key to transport. Not all molecules may pass through easily. Some molecules require energy or carrier molecules and may only cross when needed.

Passive transport does not require energy and moves the material down the concentration gradient (high to low). Small uncharged molecules may pass through the membrane in this manner. Two examples of passive transport include diffusion and osmosis. **Diffusion** is the ability of molecules to move from areas of high concentration to areas of low concentration. It normally involves small uncharged particles like oxygen. **Osmosis** is simply the diffusion of water across a semi-permeable membrane. Osmosis may cause cells to swell or shrink, depending on the internal and external environments. The following terms are used to describe the relationship of the cell to the environment.

Isotonic - Water concentration is equal inside and outside the cell. Net movement of water is basically equivalent.

Hypertonic - "Hyper" refers to the amount of dissolved particles. The more particles in a solution, the lower its water concentration will be, relative to another solution. Therefore, when a cell is hypertonic to its environment, there is a higher water concentration outside the cell than inside. Water will move into the cell and the cell will swell. If the environment is hypertonic to the cell, there is a higher water concentration inside the cell. Water will move out of the cell and the cell will shrink.

Hypotonic - "Hypo" again refers to the amount of dissolved particles. The fewer particles in solution, the higher its water concentration will be, relative to another solution. When a cell is hypotonic to its environment, there is a higher water concentration inside the cell than outside. Water will move out of the cell and the cell will shrink. If the environment is hypotonic to the cell, there is a higher water concentration outside the cell than inside. Water will move into the cell and the cell will swell.

The **facilitated diffusion** mechanism does not require energy, but does require a carrier protein. An example is insulin, which is needed to carry glucose into the cell. Facilitated diffusion can only move substances down their concentration gradient.

Active transport requires energy. The energy for this process comes from either ATP or an electrical charge difference. Active transport may move materials either with or against a concentration gradient. Some examples of active transport are:

- Sodium-Potassium pump - maintains an electrical charge across the cell membrane. This is useful in restoring ion balance so nerves can continue to function. It exchanges sodium ions for potassium ions across the plasma membrane in animal cells.

- Stomach acid pump - exports hydrogen ions to lower the pH of the stomach and increase acidity.

- Calcium pumps - actively pumps calcium outside of the cell and are important in nerve signal transmission and muscle contraction.

Active transport involves a membrane potential, which is a charge on the membrane. The charge works like a magnet and may cause transport proteins to alter their shape, moving substances into or out of the cell.

Skill 3.4 Recognizing the role of electron transport systems and ATP in respiration and photosynthesis

See Skill 2.2 and 3.2

COMPETENCY 4.0   UNDERSTAND THE PROCESSES OF CELL
                  DIVISION, GROWTH, AND DIFFERENTIATION

Skill 4.1 Comparing the processes of mitosis, meiosis, and binary fission

Bacteria reproduce by **binary fission**. This asexual process is simply the dividing of the bacterium in half. Both new organisms are genetic clones of the parent.

The purpose of eukaryotic cell division is to provide for growth and repair of body (somatic) cells and to replenish or create sex cells for reproduction. There are two forms of eukaryotic cell division: mitosis and meiosis. **Mitosis** is the division of somatic cells and **meiosis** is the division of sex cells (e.g., gametes such as eggs and sperm).

Mitosis is divided into two phases: the **mitotic (M) phase** and **interphase**. In the mitotic phase, mitosis and cytokinesis divide the genetic material and cytoplasm, respectively. This phase is the shortest phase of the cell cycle. Interphase is the stage where the cell grows and copies the genetic material in preparation for the mitotic phase. Interphase occurs in three stages of growth: the **G1** (gap 1) period, when the cell grows and metabolizes, the **S** (synthesis) period, when the cell makes new DNA, and the **G2** (gap 2) period, when the cell makes new proteins and organelles in preparation for cell division.

The mitotic phase is a continuum of change, although it is divided into five distinct stages: prophase, prometaphase, metaphase, anaphase, and telophase.

During **prophase**, the cell proceeds through the following steps continuously, without pausing. First, the chromatin condenses to become visible chromosomes. Next, the nucleolus disappears and the nuclear membrane begins to break apart. Then, mitotic spindles composed of microtubules form that will eventually pull the chromosomes apart. Finally, the cytoskeleton breaks down and the centrioles push the spindles to the poles, or opposite ends, of the cell.

During **prometaphase**, the nuclear membrane entirely fragments and the spindle microtubules interact with the chromosomes. Kinetochore fibers attach to the chromosomes at the centromere region. **Metaphase** begins when the centrosomes are at opposite ends of the cell.. The centromeres of all the chromosomes are aligned with one another down the metaphasic plate.

During **anaphase**, the centromeres split in half and homologous chromosomes separate. The chromosomes, now composed of a single chromatid, are pulled to opposite poles of the cell, with identical sets ending up at either end. The last stage of mitosis is **telophase**. Here, two nuclei form with a full set of DNA that is identical to the parent cell. The nucleoli visibly reform and the nuclear membrane reassembles. A cell plate is seen in plant cells and a cleavage furrow forms in animal cells. Finally, cytokinesis, or division of the cytoplasm and organelles, occurs, and the parent cell becomes two offspring cells.

Below is a diagram of mitosis.

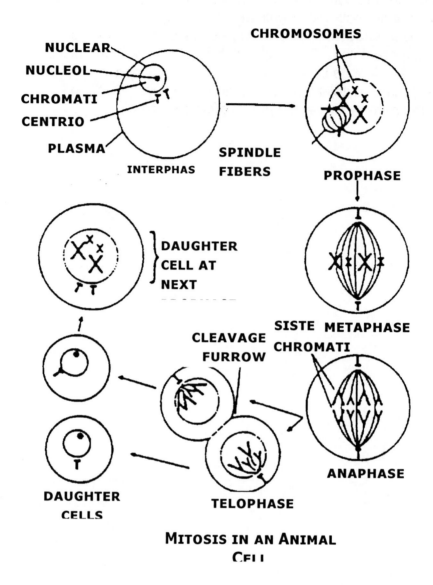

MITOSIS IN AN ANIMAL CELL

Meiosis is similar to mitosis, but, in order to reduce the chromosome number by one half, there are two consecutive cell divisions, meiosis I and meiosis II. This way, when the sperm and egg fuse during fertilization, the diploid number is maintained.

Similar to mitosis, meiosis is preceded by an interphase during which the chromosomes replicate. The steps of meiosis are as follows:

1. **Prophase I** – The replicated chromosomes condense and pair with homologues in a process called synapsis. This process forms a tetrad. Crossing over, the exchange of genetic material between homologues to further increase diversity, occurs during prophase I.
2. **Metaphase I** – The homologous pairs attach to spindle fibers after lining up in the middle of the cell.
3. **Anaphase I** – The sister chromatids remain joined and move to the poles of the cell as the homologous pairs separate.
4. **Telophase I** – The homologous chromosome pairs continue to separate. Each pole now has a haploid chromosome set. Telophase I usually occurs simultaneously with cytokinesis. In animal cells a cleavage furrow forms, and in plant cells a cell plate appears.
5. **Prophase II** – A spindle apparatus forms as the chromosomes remain condensed.
6. **Metaphase II** – Chromosomes composed of sister chromatids line up in center of cell. The centromeres divide and the sister chromatids begin to separate.
7. **Anaphase II** – The separated chromatids move to opposite ends of the cell.
8. **Telophase II** – Cytokinesis occurs, resulting in four haploid daughter cells.

Below is a diagram of meiosis.

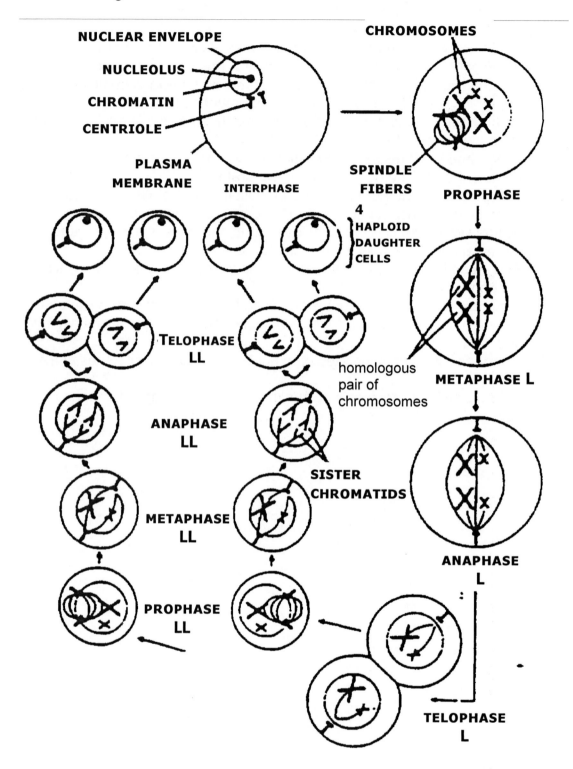

Skill 4.2 Demonstrating knowledge of the phases of the cell cycle and the effects of unregulated cell growth

See also Skill 4.1

Cells pass through restriction points in the cell cycle; the restriction point may halt cell division or allow it to proceed. The most common restriction point in the cell cycle occurs late in the G_1 phase of the cell cycle. This is when the decision whether to divide is made. If all the internal and external cell systems are working properly, the cell proceeds to divide. Cells may also decide not to proceed past the restriction point. This nondividing cell state is called the G_0 phase. Many specialized cells remain in this state.

The density of cells also regulates cell division. Density-dependent inhibition is when cells crowd one another, therefore halting cell division. Cancer cells do not respond to density-dependent inhibition. They divide excessively and invade other tissues. As long as there are nutrients, cancer cells continue to divide.

Skill 4.3 Analyzing the role of cell differentiation in the development of tissues

Differentiation is the process in which cells become specialized in structure and function. The fate of the cell is usually maintained through many subsequent generations. Gene regulatory proteins can generate many cell types during development but once a cell line differentiates it becomes permanently specialized in function. Scientists believe that gene regulatory proteins are passed to the next generation of cells to ensure the specialized expression of genes occurs.

Stem cells are not terminally differentiated. They can divide for as long as the animal is alive. When the stem cell divides, its daughter cells can either remain a stem cell or proceed with terminal differentiation. There are many types of stem cells that are specialized for different classes of terminally differentiated cells.

Embryonic stem cells give rise to all the tissues and cell types in the body. In culture, these cells have led to the creation of animal tissue that can replace damaged tissues. It is hoped that with continued research, embryonic stem cells can be cultured to replace damaged muscles, tissues, and organs.

Animal tissue becomes specialized during development. The ectoderm (outer layer) of the developing embryo becomes the epidermis or skin. The mesoderm (middle layer) becomes muscles and other organs beside the gut. The endoderm (inner layer) becomes the gut, also called the archenteron.

Skill 4.4 Analyzing factors (e.g., genetics, disease, nutrition, exposure to toxic substances) that influence cell division and differentiation

Environmental factors can influence the structure and expression of genes, and thus can influence cell division and differentiation. For instance, viruses can insert their DNA into the host's genome changing the composition of the host DNA. In addition, mutagenic agents found in the environment can cause mutations in DNA and carcinogenic agents promote cancer, often by causing DNA mutations.

Many viruses can insert their DNA into the host genome causing mutations. Many times, viral insertion of DNA does not harm the host DNA because of the location of the insertion. Some insertions, however, can have grave consequences for the host. Oncogenes are genes that increase the malignancy of tumor cells. Some viruses carry oncogenes that, when inserted into the host genome, become active and promote cancerous growth. In addition, insertion of other viral DNA into the host genome can stimulate expression of host proto-oncogenes, genes that normally promote cell division. For example, insertion of a strong viral promoter in front of a host proto-oncogene may stimulate expression of the gene and lead to uncontrolled cell growth (i.e. cancer).

In addition to viruses, physical and chemical agents found in the environment can damage gene structure. Mutagenic agents cause mutations in DNA. Examples of mutagenic agents are x-rays, ultraviolet light, and ethidium bromide. Carcinogenic agents are any substances that promote cancer. Carcinogens are often, but not always, mutagens. Examples of agents carcinogenic to humans are asbestos, ultraviolet light, x-rays, and benzene.

COMPETENCY 5.0   UNDERSTAND THE PRINCIPLES OF HEREDITY

Skill 5.1 Applying knowledge of the laws of probability to determine genotypic and phenotypic frequencies in Mendelian inheritance

Gregor Mendel is generally recognized as the father of genetics. His work in the late 1800's forms the basis of our knowledge of genetics. Although unaware of the presence of DNA or genes, Mendel realized there were factors (now known as **genes**) that were transferred from parents to their offspring. Mendel worked with pea plants and fertilized the plants himself, keeping track of the traits of subsequent generations which led to the Mendelian laws of genetics. Mendel found that two "factors" governed each trait, one factor being inherited from each parent. Traits or characteristics came in several forms, known as **alleles**. For example, the trait of flower color had white alleles (*p*) and purple alleles (*P*). Mendel formulated two laws: the law of segregation and the law of independent assortment.

The **law of segregation** states that only one of the two possible alleles from each parent is passed on to the offspring. If the two alleles differ, then one is fully expressed in the organism's appearance (the dominant allele) and the other has no noticeable effect on appearance (the recessive allele). The two alleles for each trait segregate into different gametes. A Punnett square can be used to illustrate the law of segregation. In a Punnett square, one parent's genes are put at the top of the box and the other parent's on the side. Genes combine in the squares just like numbers are added in addition tables. This Punnett square shows the possible result of the cross of two F$_1$ hybrids.

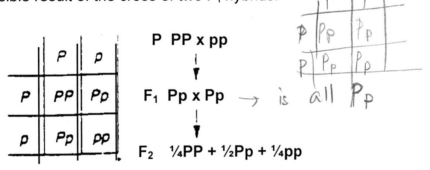

This cross results in a 1:2:1 ratio of F$_2$ offspring. Here, the dominant allele is indicated by *P* and the recessive allele is indicated by *p*. The F$_1$ cross results in three-quarters of all offspring expressing the dominant allele (one half with *PP* and one quarter with *Pp*) and one-quarter of all offspring expressing the recessive allele (*pp*). Some other important terms to know:

Homozygous – having a pair of identical alleles. For example, *PP* and *pp* are homozygous pairs.
Heterozygous – having two different alleles. For example, *Pp* is a heterozygous pair.

Phenotype – the organism's physical appearance. For example, a purple flower. **Genotype** – the organism's genetic makeup. For example, *PP* and *Pp* have the same phenotype (purple in color), but different genotypes.

The **law of independent assortment** states that alleles assort independently of each other. The law of segregation applies for monohybrid crosses (a cross in which only one characteristic is observed). In a dihybrid cross, two characteristics are observed simultaneously. Two of the seven characters Mendel studied were seed shape and color. Yellow is the dominant seed color (*Y*) and green is the recessive color (*y*). The dominant seed shape is round (*R*) and the recessive shape is wrinkled (*r*). A cross between a plant with yellow round seeds (*YYRR*) and a plant with green wrinkled seeds (*yyrr*) produces an F_1 generation with the genotype *YyRr*. The production of F_2 offspring, from an F_1 x F_1 cross, results in a 9:3:3:1 phenotypic ratio.

F_2

	YR	Yr	yR	yr
YR	YYRR	YYRr	YyRR	YyRr
Yr	YYRr	YYrr	YyRr	Yyrr
yR	YyRR	YyRr	yyRR	yyRr
yr	YyRr	Yyrr	yyRr	yyrr

P   YYRR x yyrr

↓

F_1 YyRr

↓

F_2
YYRR – 1 ⎫
YYRr – 2 ⎬ 9 yellow round
YyRR – 2 ⎪
YyRr – 4 ⎭

yyRR – 1 ⎫
yyRr – 2 ⎬ 3 green round

YYrr – 1 ⎫
Yyrr – 2 ⎬ 3 yellow wrinkled

yyrr – 1 ⎫ 1 green wrinkled

Based on Mendelian genetics, the more complex hereditary pattern of **dominance** was discovered. In Mendel's law of segregation, the F_1 generation have either purple or white flowers. This is an example of **complete dominance**. **Incomplete dominance** is when the F_1 generation results in an appearance somewhere between the two parents. For example, red flowers are crossed with white flowers, resulting in an F_1 generation with pink flowers. The red and white traits are still carried by the F_1 generation, resulting in an F_2 generation with a phenotypic ratio of 1:2:1 (for red, pink, and white flowers, respectively). In **codominance,** two or more alleles may be equally dominant while other alleles are recessive. The ABO blood grouping is an example of codominance. Type A and Type B are of equal strength, and are said to be codominant, while Type O is recessive. Therefore, an individual with Type A blood may have the genotypes of AA or AO; an individual with Type B blood may have the genotypes of BB or BO; an individual with Type AB blood has the genotype AB; and an individual with Type O blood has the genotype OO.

Skill 5.2 Demonstrating knowledge of the relationship of the behavior of chromosomes during meiosis and fertilization to inheritance patterns

Each chromosome, of which there are 46 (two pairs of 23) in humans, contains genes. Genes are the basic units of inheritance. In humans, chromosomal inheritance determines the sex of the individual. A woman's sex is denoted as XX, and the mother always donates an X chromosome to her child. The male sex is denoted as XY, and the father can pass either an X or Y chromosome to his offspring. It is the paring of maternal and paternal sex chromosomes that determines the sex of the baby. It is also true that a parent passes on other genes influencing phenotype such as genes influencing eye color, height, and physique. Chromosomal aberrations—changes in either the total number of chromosomes or the molecular structure of chromosomes—may lead to physical abnormalities in the offspring. For example, an extra copy of chromosome 21 causes Down syndrome.

Meiosis and fertilization generate genetic diversity. There are several mechanisms that contribute to genetic variation in sexual reproductive organisms. Three of them are independent assortment of chromosomes, crossing over, and random fertilization.

Skill 5.3 Recognizing factors influencing the transmission of genes from one generation to the next (e.g., linkage, position of gene on a chromosome, crossing over, independent assortment)

At the metaphase I stage of meiosis, each homologous pair of chromosomes is situated along the metaphase plate. The orientation of the homologous pair is random and independent of the other pairs of metaphase I. This results in an **independent assortment** of maternal and paternal chromosomes. Based on this information, it seems as though each chromosome in a gamete would be of only maternal or paternal origin. However, a process called crossing over prevents this from happening.

Crossing over occurs during prophase I. At this point, nonsister chromatids from each homologous pair exchange corresponding segments. Crossing over results in the combination of DNA from both parents, allowing for greater genetic variation in sexual life cycles.

Non-Mendelian inheritance is a general term describing any pattern of genetic inheritance that does not conform to Mendel's basic laws or does not rely on a single chromosomal gene. Examples of non-Mendelian inheritance include polygenic traits, environmental influence, organelle DNA, transmission bias, and epigenetics.

Multiple genes determine the expression of polygenic traits. For example, disorders arising from a defect in a single gene are rare compared to complex disorders like cancer, heart disease, and diabetes. The inheritance of such complex disorders does not follow Mendelian rules because they involve more than one gene.

While chromosomal DNA carries the majority of an organism's genetic material, organelles, including mitochondria and chloroplasts, also have DNA containing genes. Organelle genes have their own patterns of inheritance that do not conform to Mendelian rules. Such patterns of inheritance are often called maternal because offspring receive all of their organelle DNA from the mother.

Transmission bias describes a situation in which the alleles of the parent organisms are not equally represented in their offspring. Transmission bias often results from the failure of alleles to segregate properly during cell division. Mendelian genetics assumes equal representation of parent alleles in the offspring generation.

Epigenetic inheritance involves changes not involving DNA sequence. For example, the addition of methyl groups (methylation) to DNA molecules can influence the expression of genes and override Mendelian patterns of inheritance.

Finally, genetic linkage (defined below) is often considered a form of non-Mendelian inheritance because closely linked chromosomal genes tend to assort together, not separately. Linkage, however, is not entirely non-Mendelian because classical genetics can generally explain and predict the patterns of inheritance of linked genes.

Genetic linkage is the inheritance of two or more traits together. In general, the transmission of a particular allele is independent of the alleles passed on for other traits. This inheritance pattern appears to violate Mendelian genetics because genes found on the same chromosome often remain together during meiosis. Thus, these linked genes have a great probability of being inherited together by offspring.

The phenomenon known as crossing over prevents complete linkage of genes on the same chromosome. During meiosis, paired chromosomes exchange genetic material creating new combinations of DNA. Crossing over is more likely to disrupt linkage when genes are far apart on a chromosome. Greater distance between genes increases the probability that crossing over will occur between the gene loci.

Skill 5.4 Recognizing how the genotype of an organism influences the expression of traits in its phenotype (e.g., dominant and recessive traits, polygenic inheritance, genetic disorders)

You will recall that we discussed earlier the **law of segregation** (review Skill 5.1), which states that each parent passes to the offspring only one of two possible alleles. If the two alleles present in a diploid organism differ, then one is fully expressed in the organism's appearance (the dominant allele) and the other has no noticeable effect on appearance (the recessive allele). Most people with recessive disorders are born to parents with normal phenotypes. The mating of heterozygous parents would result in an offspring genotypic ratio of 1:2:1; thus 1 out of 4 offspring would by homozygous recessive, and express this recessive trait. The heterozygous parents are called carriers because they do not express the trait phenotypically but pass the trait on to their offspring.

Lethal dominant alleles are much less common than lethal recessive alleles. This is because lethal dominant alleles are not masked in heterozygotes. Mutations in a gene of the sperm or egg can result in a lethal dominant allele, but this is usually fatal to the developing embryo.

Sex linked traits - the Y chromosome found only in males (XY) carries little genetic information, whereas the X chromosome found in females (XX) carries a significant amount of genetic information. Since males have no second X chromosome potentially to mask a recessive gene, the recessive trait is expressed more often in men. Women must have the recessive gene on both X chromosomes to express the trait. Examples of sex linked traits include hemophilia and color-blindness.

Sex influenced traits – some traits are influenced by the sex hormones. Male pattern baldness is an example of a sex influenced trait. Testosterone influences the expression of the gene.

Nondisjunction - during meiosis, chromosomes may fail to separate properly. One sex cell may get both chromosomes and another may get none. While this is usually fatal to the gamete itself or the developing zygote, some combinations are not uniformly fatal. An example of nondisjunction is found in Down Syndrome, where an extra copy of the twenty-first chromosome is present; the condition is also known as Trisomy-21.

Skill 5.5 Analyzing effects of environmental factors (e.g., light, nutrition, moisture, temperature) on the expression of traits in the phenotype of an organism

An individual organism's phenotype is its physical appearance. Thus, the term phenotype may refer to the individual's overall physical form or to the physical manifestation of a single trait. While it is commonly said in biology that the phenotype is simply the outward expression of the genotype, this is not the whole story. First, there is a certain degree of random variation that occurs. This means that even if two genetically identical organisms were raised under identical conditions, there could be differences in their phenotypes. Second, there is a complex interplay between the environment and genotype that ultimately decides an individual phenotype.

The change of phenotype in response to environmental conditions is known as phenotypic plasticity. Phenotypic plasticity is what allows individuals with identical genotypes to respond to their unique environments in unique ways. Note that the degree of plasticity varies widely between various species and specific traits. The pattern of phenotypic expression that results from the interaction of a given genotype with varying environments is known as the norm of reaction. The norm of reaction for a certain genotype may be two or more discrete and distinct phenotypes (an example is offered below). Alternatively, the norm of reaction may be continuous and consist of a range of fairly similar phenotypes. An example of this is human height, which can be any of a continuous range of values and depends on both genetics and nutrition. Note how plasticity of phenotype may be an advantage to an organism, as it allows it to adapt to varying environmental conditions.

We can easily think of examples in which individual plant and animal phenotypes have been altered by lack or surplus of water, light, and/or adequate nutrition. Examples of physical traits that are known to be especially plastic include leaf morphology, color of fur or hair, height and limb length, and more complex behavioral patterns. Additionally, there are several dramatic examples of this phenomenon known to science. One such case is that of social insects, such as bees. In bee communities, there are several different castes, including workers, guards, and queens. The behaviors and appearances of individuals in the various castes can vary widely. However, these differences do not arise from different genetic make-up, but from differences in the embryonic diet and incubation temperature. The interaction of genes and environment has been the subject of much research. This interaction is also the basis for the classic, if somewhat simplistic, "nature vs. nurture" debate regarding human behavior.

COMPETENCY 6.0   UNDERSTAND THE MOLECULAR BASIS OF GENETICS AND GENETIC ENGINEERING

Skill 6.1 Identifying the structures and functions of DNA and RNA in organisms

See Skill 2.4

Skill 6.2 Analyzing the mechanisms of replication, transcription, and translation

DNA replicates semi-conservatively; this means the two original strands are conserved and serve as templates for the two new strands.

The first step in DNA replication is the unwinding of the supercoiled strands. An enzyme called **helicase** unwinds the DNA as the replication fork proceeds and **topoisomerases** relieve the tension by nicking one strand and relaxing the supercoil.

Once the strands have separated, they must be stabilized. Single-strand binding proteins (SSBs) bind to the single strands until the DNA is replicated.
An RNA polymerase called primase adds ribonucleotides to the DNA template to initiate DNA synthesis. This short RNA-DNA hybrid is called a **primer**. Once the DNA is single stranded, **DNA polymerases** add nucleotides in the 5' → 3' direction.

As DNA synthesis proceeds along the replication fork, it becomes obvious that replication is semi-discontinuous in one direction; meaning one strand is synthesized in the direction the replication fork is opening and the other strand is synthesized in the opposite direction. The continuously synthesized strand is the **leading strand** and the discontinuously synthesized strand is the **lagging strand**. As the replication fork proceeds, new primer is added to the lagging strand and it is synthesized discontinuously, in a direction opposite to the opening of the replication fork, in small fragments called **Okazaki fragments**.

The RNA primers that remain after replication must be removed and replaced with deoxyribonucleotides. DNA polymerase has 5' → 3' polymerase activity and has 3' → 5' exonuclease activity. This enzyme binds to the nick between the Okazaki fragment and the RNA primer. It removes the primer and adds deoxyribonucleotides in the 5' → 3' direction. The nick still remains until **DNA ligase** seals it, producing the final product, a double-stranded segment of DNA.

Once the double-stranded segment is replicated a proofreading process is carried out by DNA replication enzymes. In eukaryotes, DNA polymerases have 3' → 5' exonuclease activity—they move backwards and remove nucleotides where the enzyme recognizes an error, then add the correct nucleotide in the 5' → 3' direction. In *E. coli*, DNA polymerase II synthesizes DNA during repair of DNA damage.

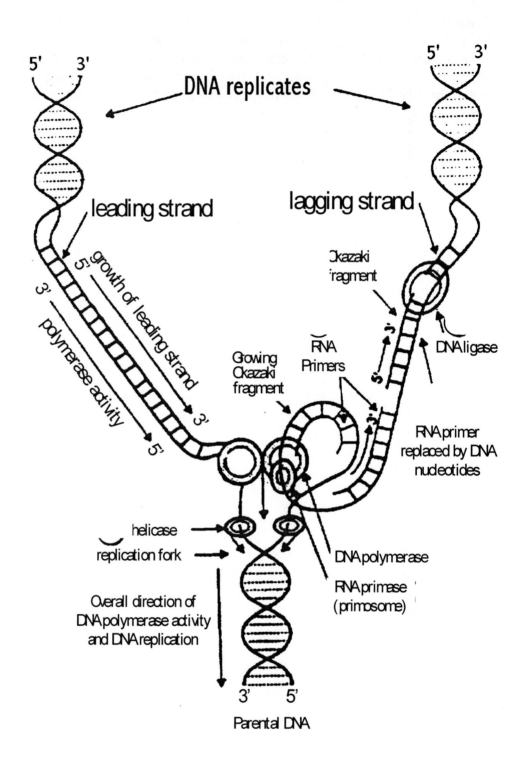

Protein synthesis

Proteins are synthesized through the processes of transcription and translation. Three major classes of RNA are needed to carry out these processes: messenger RNA (mRNA), ribosomal RNA (rRNA), and transfer RNA (tRNA). **Messenger RNA** contains information for translation; **ribosomal RNA** is a structural component of the ribosome; and **transfer RNA** carries amino acids to the ribosome for protein synthesis.

Transcription is similar in prokaryotes and eukaryotes. During transcription, the DNA molecule is copied, or transcribed, into an RNA molecule (mRNA). Transcription occurs through the steps of initiation, elongation, and termination. Transcription also occurs for rRNA and tRNA, but the focus here is on mRNA.

Initiation begins at the promoter of the double-stranded DNA molecule. The promoter is a specific region of DNA that directs the **RNA polymerase** to bind to the DNA at that point. The double-stranded DNA opens up and RNA polymerase begins transcription in the 5' → 3' direction by pairing ribonucleotides to the deoxyribonucleotides as follows to get a complementary mRNA segment:

Deoxyribonucleotide		Ribonucleotide
A	→	U
G	→	C

Elongation is the synthesis on the mRNA strand in the 5' → 3' direction. The new mRNA rapidly separates from the DNA template and the complementary DNA strands pair together again.

Termination of transcription occurs at the end of a gene or sequence of genes. Cleavage, or cutting, occurs at specific sites on the mRNA. This process is aided by termination factors.

In eukaryotes, mRNA goes through **posttranscriptional processing** before going on to translation.

There are three basic steps of posttranscriptional processing:

1. **5' capping** – The addition of a methylated base to protects the 5' end from degradation. The cap also serves as the site where ribosomes bind to the mRNA for translation
2. **3' polyadenylation** – The addition of 100-300 adenine bases to the free 3' end of mRNA resulting in a poly-A-tail
3. **Intron removal**- The removal of non-coding introns and the splicing together of coding exons, to form the mature mRNA

Translation is the process in which the mRNA sequence is read in order to create a polypeptide. The mRNA sequence determines the amino acid sequence of a protein by following a pattern called the genetic code. The **genetic code** consists of 64 mRNA triplet nucleotide combinations called **codons**. Three codons are termination (e.g. "stop") codons and the remaining 61 code for specific amino acids. mRNA codes for 20 amino acids, the building blocks of protein. They are attached together by peptide bonds to form a polypeptide chain.

Ribosomes are the site of translation. They contain rRNA and protein. Translation occurs in three steps: initiation, elongation, and termination. Initiation occurs when the methylated tRNA binds to the ribosome to form a complex. This complex then binds to the 5' cap of the mRNA. In elongation, individual tRNA molecules carry an amino acid to the ribosome and place it in order, determined by the mRNA sequence. tRNA is specific–it only accepts one of the 20 amino acids that corresponds to the anticodon. The anticodon is complementary to the codon. For example, using the codon sequence below:

The mRNA codons are: A U G   / G A G   / C A U   / G C U   / . . .
The tRNA anticodons are: U A C   / C U C   / G U A   / C G A   / . . .
The amino acids are: Met   / Glu   / His   / Ala   / . . .

Termination occurs when the ribosome reaches any one of the three stop codons: UAA, UAG, or UGA. The newly formed polypeptide then undergoes posttranslational modification to alter or remove portions of the polypeptide, as appropriate.

Skill 6.3 Demonstrating knowledge of the characteristics of the genetic code

Cells read the base sequence of genes three at a time. A three base sequence, called a codon, codes for a specific amino acid that specialized proteins attach to the growing polypeptide chain. Four bases taken three at a time produces 64 possible combinations (4 x 4 x 4), more than enough to code for the 20 amino acids. Thus, an amino acid may have from one to six triplet codons that code for it. In addition, three of the codons are stop codons that cause termination of transcription rather than coding for an amino acid.

The genetic code has several important characteristics. First, the code is unambiguous as each codon specifies only one amino acid. Second, the code is redundant as more than one codon may code for a single amino acid. Third, in most cases the third base in a codon plays only a minor role in amino acid recognition and coding. For example, the four codons for alanine all start with GC (GCC, GCA, GCT, and GCG). Fourth, in general codons with similar sequences code for amino acids with similar chemical properties. Finally, the AUG codon that codes for methionine is also a transcription start codon—thus all polypeptide chains begin with methionine, though it may later be removed.

It is also important to note that different organisms show different statistical preferences for the use of triplet codons and amino acids. This characteristic is important when attempting to transfer genes between species.

Skill 6.4 Analyzing types of mutations and their consequences

Inheritable changes in DNA are called mutations. **Mutations** may be errors in replication or a spontaneous rearrangement of one or more segments of DNA by factors like radioactivity, drugs, or chemicals. The severity of the change is not as critical as where the change occurs. DNA contains large segments of non-coding areas called introns. The important coding areas are called exons. If an error occurs on an intron, there is no effect on the organism's phenotype. If the error occurs on an exon, it may have an impact on the phenotype ranging from minor to lethal, depending on the severity of the mistake. Mutations may occur on somatic or sex cells. Usually the mutations on sex cells are more dangerous since they contain the basis of all future information for a developing offspring. But mutations are not always bad. They are the basis of evolution and if they create a favorable variation that enhances the organism's survival they are beneficial. But mutations may also lead to abnormalities, birth defects, and even death. There are several types of mutations.

A **point mutation** is a mutation involving a single nucleotide or a few adjacent nucleotides. Let's suppose a normal sequence was as follows:

Normal sequence	A B C D E F
Duplication (a nucleotide is repeated)	A B C C D E F
Inversion (a segment is reversed)	A E D C B F
Insertion or **Translocation** (a segment of DNA is put in the wrong location)	A B C R S D E F
Breakage (a segment is lost)	A B F (CDE lost)

Deletion and insertion mutations that shift the reading frame are **frame shift mutations**; that is, all codons from that point forward will be read incorrectly.

A **silent mutation** makes no change in the amino acid sequence and therefore does not alter the protein produced. A **missense mutation** results in an alteration in the amino acid sequence. A mutation's effect on protein function depends on which amino acids are involved and how many are involved. The structure of a protein usually determines its function. A mutation that does not alter the structure will probably have little or no effect on the protein's function. However, a mutation that does alter the structure of a protein and can severely impact protein activity is called a **loss-of-function mutation**. Sickle-cell anemia and cystic fibrosis are examples of loss-of-function mutations.

Sickle-cell anemia is characterized by weakness, heart failure, joint and muscular impairment, fatigue, abdominal pain and dysfunction, impaired mental function, and eventual death. The mutation that causes this genetic disorder is a point mutation in the sixth amino acid of hemoglobin. A normal hemoglobin molecule has glutamic acid as the sixth amino acid while the sickle-cell hemoglobin has valine at the sixth position. This mutation causes the chemical properties of hemoglobin to change. The hemoglobin of a sickle-cell person has a lower affinity for oxygen, causing red blood cells to have a sickle shape. The sickle shape of the red blood cell causes the formation of clumps of cells and capillary blockage because the cells do not pass through capillaries well.

Cystic fibrosis is the most common genetic disorder among people of European ancestry. This disorder disrupts the exocrine system. Fibrous cysts form on the pancreas, blocking the pancreatic ducts. Sweat glands release high levels of salt. Thick mucous accumulates in the lungs. The accumulation of mucous facilitates bacterial infection and possible death. Cystic fibrosis cannot be cured but its symptoms can be treated. Many children with the disorder die before adulthood. Scientists have identified a protein that transports chloride ions across cell membranes; individuals with cystic fibrosis have a mutation in the gene coding for this protein. The majority of the mutant alleles have a deletion of the three nucleotides coding for phenylalanine at position 508. Other people with the disorder have mutant alleles caused by substitution, deletion, and frameshifts.

Skill 6.5 Demonstrating knowledge of extranuclear inheritance (e.g., mitochondrial DNA)

Mitochondrial DNA passed to offspring is donated only by the mother. A genetic defect in the mother's mitochondrial DNA will pass to her offspring, regardless of the father's mitochondrial DNA.

Skill 6.6 Recognizing techniques used in the isolation, manipulation, and expression of genetic material (e.g., electrophoresis, DNA forensics, recombinant DNA technology)

In its simplest form, genetic engineering requires enzymes to cut DNA, a vector for genetic material, and a target host organism to receive the recombinant DNA. A **restriction enzyme** is a bacterial enzyme that cuts foreign DNA in specific locations. The restricted fragment that results can be inserted into a bacterial plasmid (a **vector**). Viruses are also sometimes used as vectors. The splicing of restricted fragments into a plasmid vector results in a recombinant plasmid. This recombinant plasmid can then be placed in a host cell, usually a bacterial cell, for replication.

The use of recombinant DNA provides a means to move genes between species. This opens the door for cloning specific genes of interest. Hybridization can be used to find a gene of interest. A probe is a molecule complementary in sequence to the gene of interest. The probe can be detected by labeling with a radioactive isotope or a fluorescent tag—this makes it easy to locate the probe, hence the gene of interest, once the probe has bonded to the target gene.

Gel electrophoresis is another method used for DNA analysis. Electrophoresis separates DNA or protein by size or electrical charge. DNA moves toward a positive charge and the DNA fragments separate by size as they move through a thick gel substrate. The gel is treated with a DNA-binding dye that fluoresces under ultraviolet light. A picture of the gel can be taken and used for analysis; the picture will illustrate the various size of DNA fragments present in the source material.

One of the most widely used genetic engineering techniques is **polymerase chain reaction (PCR)**. PCR is a technique in which a piece of DNA can be amplified into billions of copies within a few hours. This process requires a primer to specify the segment to be copied, and an enzyme (usually taq polymerase) to amplify the DNA. PCR has allowed scientists to perform multiple procedures on small amounts of DNA.

Forensic scientists can use DNA technology to solve crimes. In some cases, DNA testing can determine a person's guilt or innocence. A suspect's "DNA fingerprint" is compared to DNA samples collected from a crime scene. If the fingerprint matches the samples, guilt may be inferred.

Skill 6.7 Recognizing applications of genetic engineering in medicine (e.g., gene therapy) and agriculture (e.g., transgenic organisms)

Genetic engineering has made enormous contributions to medicine and has opened the door to DNA technology.

The use of DNA probes and polymerase chain reaction (PCR) has enabled scientists to identify and detect elusive pathogens. Diagnosis of genetic disease sometimes is possible before the onset of symptoms.

Genetic engineering has allowed for the treatment of some genetic disorders. **Gene therapy** is the introduction of a normal allele to the somatic cells to replace the defective allele. The medical field has had success in treating patients with a single enzyme deficiency disease. Gene therapy has allowed doctors and scientists to introduce a normal allele that would provide the missing enzyme.

Gene-splicing techniques have allowed human insulin and human growth hormones to be produced by bacteria. Insulin treatment helps control diabetes for millions of people who suffer from the disease. The insulin produced in genetically engineered bacteria is chemically identical to that made in the human pancreas. Human growth hormone (HGH) has been genetically engineered for the treatment of dwarfism caused by insufficient amounts of HGH. HGH is being further researched for treatment of broken bones and severe burns.

Biotechnology has advanced the techniques used to create vaccines. Genetic engineering allows for the modification of a pathogen in order to attenuate it for vaccine use. In fact, vaccines created from pathogens attenuated by gene-splicing may be safer than those that use more traditional methods.

Many microorganisms are used to detoxify toxic chemicals and to recycle waste. Sewage treatment plants use microbes to degrade organic compounds. Some compounds, like chlorinated hydrocarbons, cannot be easily degraded. Scientists are working on ways to genetically modify microbes to allow them to degrade harmful compounds.

Genetic engineering has benefited agriculture also. For example, many dairy cows are given bovine growth hormone to increase milk production. Commercially grown plants are often genetically modified for optimal growth.

Strains of wheat, cotton, and soybeans have been developed to resist herbicides used to control weeds. This allows for the successful growth of the plants while destroying the weeds. Crop plants are also being engineered to resist infections and pests. Scientists can genetically modify crops to contain a viral gene that allegedly does not alter the plant but will "vaccinate" the plant from a virus attack. Crop plants are now being modified to resist insect attacks. This presumably will allow farmers to reduce the amount of pesticide used on plants.

Skill 6.8 Demonstrating knowledge of ethical issues related to research in genetics and genetic engineering

Genetic engineering has drastically advanced the science of biotechnology. With these advancements come concerns about safety and ethics. Many safety concerns have been addressed by strict government regulations. The FDA, USDA, EPA, and NIH are just a few of the United States governmental agencies that regulate pharmaceutical, food, and environmental technologies.

Several ethical questions arise when discussing biotechnology. Should embryonic stem cell research be allowed? Is animal testing humane? These are just a couple of ethical questions that many people have. There are strong arguments for both sides of each issue and there are some governmental regulations in place to monitor these issues.

Concepts that reflect a person's ethics may be used for political purposes, either to further one's agenda, or to hurt an opponent. Recent political issues with ethical and scientific ties include abortion, stem cell research, and human cloning. There are at least two sides to each issue and as such they can easily become partisan in nature. This partisan delineation of a topic can impact elections. Local, state, national, and global governments and organizations must increasingly consider policy issues related to science and technology. For example, local and state governments must analyze the impact of proposed development and growth on the environment. Governments and communities must balance the demands of an expanding human population with the local ecology to ensure sustainable growth.

COMPETENCY 7.0   UNDERSTAND PRINCIPLES OF TAXONOMY AND CLASSIFICATION IN BIOLOGY

Skill 7.1 Demonstrating knowledge of characteristics of biological classification (i.e., hierarchy of taxonomic levels, importance of heritable characteristics in classifying organisms) and recognizing the procedures and criteria used to classify organisms

Scientists estimate that there are more than ten million different species of living things. Of these, 1.5 million have been named and classified by science. Systems of classification show similarities between organisms and assist scientists with a worldwide system of organization.

Carolus Linnaeus is termed the father of **taxonomy,** the science of classification. Linnaeus based his system on morphology (study of structure). Later, evolutionary relationships (phylogeny) were also used to sort and group species. The modern classification system uses binomial nomenclature, a two-part name, for every species. The genus is the first part of the name and the species is the second part. For example, *Homo sapiens* is the scientific name for the human species. In an expanded classification system, all organisms are placed in several levels of organization—starting with kingdom, each level of group gets smaller, and generally included organisms are more alike, as one moves down the levels in the classification. For example, the human species can be fully classified as:

Kingdom: Animalia; Phylum: Chordata (Subphylum: Vertebrata); Class: Mammalia; Order: Primate; Family: Hominidae; Genus: Homo; Species: sapiens.

One common definition of a species suggests that organisms are members of the same species if they are able to successfully reproduce with each other.

Several different morphological criteria are used to classify organisms:

1   **Ancestral characteristics** - characteristics that are inherited from a common ancestor (e.g. 5 digits on the hand of an ape)
2   **Derived characteristics** - characteristics that have evolved more recently (e.g. the absence of a tail on an ape)
3   **Conservative characteristics** - traits that change slowly
4   **Homologous characteristics** - characteristics with the same genetic basis, but used for a different function. (e.g., wing of a bat, arm of a human. The bone structure is the same, but the limbs are used for different purposes)
5.   **Analogous characteristics** – structures that differ in construction, but used for similar purposes (e.g. the wing of a bird and the wing of a butterfly)
6.   **Convergent evolution** - development of similar environmental adaptations by organisms that are genetically unrelated

Molecular characteristics are also used to classify organisms. Protein comparison, DNA comparison, and analysis of fossilized DNA are powerful comparative methods used to measure evolutionary relationships between species. Taxonomists consider the organism's life history, biochemical (DNA) makeup, behavior, and geographical distribution. The fossil record is also used to show evolutionary relationships.

Skill 7.2 Demonstrating knowledge of the taxonomic relationships among organisms

The typical graphic product of a classification effort is a **phylogenetic tree**, which represents a hypothesis of the relationships of sub-groups within a larger group, based on branching of lineages through time.

Every time you see a phylogenetic tree, you should be aware that it is making statements on the degree of similarity between organisms, or the particular pattern in which the various lineages diverged (phylogenetic history).

Cladistics is the study of phylogenetic relationships of organisms by analysis of shared, derived character states. Cladograms are constructed to show evolutionary pathways. Character states are polarized in cladistic analysis to be plesiomorphous (ancestral features), symplesiomorphous (shared ancestral features), apomorphous (derived features), and synapomorphous (shared, derived features).

Skill 7.3 Identifying distinguishing characteristics of taxonomic groups at the domain and kingdom levels

The traditional classification of all living things uses a five-kingdom system. The five kingdoms are Monera, Protista, Fungi, Plantae, and Animalia. The following is a comparison of the cellular characteristics of members of the five kingdoms.

Kingdom Monera

Members of Kingdom Monera are single-celled, prokaryotic organisms. Like all prokaryotes, Monerans lack nuclei and other membrane bound organelles, but do contain circular chromosomes and ribosomes. Most Monerans possess a cell wall made of peptidoglycan, a combination of sugars and proteins. Some Monerans also possess capsules and external motility devices (e.g. pili or flagella). The Kingdom Monera includes both eubacteria and archaebacteria. Though archaebacteria are structurally similar to eubacteria in many ways, there are key differences, like cell wall structure (archaebacteria lack peptidoglycan).

Kingdom Protista

Protists are eukaryotic, usually single-celled organisms (though some protists are multicellular). The Kingdom Protista is very diverse, containing members with some characteristics of plants, animals, and fungi. All protists possess nuclei and some types of protists possess multiple nuclei. Most protists contain many mitochondria for energy production, and photosynthetic protists contain specialized structures called plastids where photosynthesis occurs. Motile protists possess external cilia or flagella. Finally, many protists have cell walls that do not contain cellulose.

Kingdom Fungi

Fungi are eukaryotic organisms that are mostly multicellular (single-celled yeast are the exception) and often multi-nucleate. Fungi possess cell walls composed of chitin. Fungal organelles are similar to animal organelles. Fungi are non-photosynthetic and possess neither chloroplasts nor plastids. Many fungal cells, like animal cells, possess centrioles. Fungi are also non-motile and release exoenzymes into the environment to dissolve food.

Kingdom Plantae

Plants are eukaryotic, multicellular, and often have cube-shaped cells. Plant cells possess rigid cell walls composed mostly of cellulose. Plant cells also contain chloroplasts and plastids for photosynthesis. Plant cells generally do not possess centrioles. Another distinguishing characteristic of plant cells is the presence of a large, central vacuole that occupies 50-90% of the cell interior.

The vacuole stores acids, sugars, waste, and water. Because of the presence of the vacuole, the cytoplasmic volume is limited.

Kingdom Animalia

Animals are eukaryotic, multicellular, and often motile. Animal cells do not possess cell walls or plastids, but do possess a complex system of organelles. Most animal cells also possess centrioles, microtubule structures that play a role in spindle formation during replication.

The three-domain system of classification, introduced by Carl Woese in 1990, emphasizes the separation of the two types of prokaryotes. The following is a comparison of the cellular characteristics of members of the three domains of living organisms: Eukarya, Bacteria, and Archaea.

Domain Eukarya

The Eukarya domain includes all members of the protist, fungi, plant, and animal kingdoms. Eukaryotic cells possess a membrane bound nucleus and other membranous organelles (e.g., mitochondria, Golgi apparatus, ribosomes). The chromosomes of Eukarya are linear and usually complexed with histones (protein spools). The cell membranes of eukaryotes consist of glycerol-ester lipids and sterols. The ribosomes of eukaryotes are 80 Svedburg (S) units in size. Finally, the cell walls of those eukaryotes that have them (i.e., plants, algae, fungi) are polysaccharide in nature.

Domain Bacteria

Prokaryotic members of the Kingdom Monera not classified as Archaea, are members of the Bacteria domain. Bacteria lack a defined nucleus and other membranous organelles. The ribosomes of bacteria measure 70 S units in size. The chromosome of Bacteria is usually a single, circular molecule that is not complexed with histones. The cell membranes of Bacteria lack sterols and consist of glycerol-ester lipids. Finally, most Bacteria possess a cell wall made of peptidoglycan.

Domain Archaea

Members of the Archaea domain are prokaryotic and similar to bacteria in most aspects of cell structure and metabolism. However, transcription and translation in Archaea are similar to the processes of eukaryotes, not bacteria. In addition, the cell membranes of Archaea consist of glycerol-ether lipids in contrast to the glycerol-ester lipids of eukaryotic and bacterial membranes. Finally, the cell walls of Archaea are not made of peptidoglycan, but consist of other polysaccharides, protein, and glycoprotein.

Skill 7.4 Demonstrating knowledge of the relationship between taxonomic classification and evolutionary history and identifying taxonomically useful traits (e.g., homologous traits) and those that are not (e.g., analogous traits)

The current five-kingdom system separates prokaryotes from eukaryotes. The prokaryotes belong to the Kingdom Monera while the eukaryotes belong to Kingdoms Protista, Plantae, Fungi, or Animalia. Recent comparisons of nucleic acids and proteins between different groups of organisms have led to problems concerning the five-kingdom system. Based on these comparisons, alternative kingdom systems have emerged. Six and eight kingdom systems as well as a three-domain system have been proposed as more accurate classification systems. It is important to note that classification systems evolve as more information regarding characteristics and evolutionary histories of organisms is discovered.

Evolutionary taxonomy classifies groups according to the course of evolution. It states that the process of evolution produces natural groups of classification. The similarities of the natural groups are due to common ancestry, which we can only infer, not observe. We infer similarities by noting the sharing of characters, not only due to common ancestry but also due to convergence. Evolutionary taxonomists have to differentiate between these two types of similarities. They have to identify homologies (ancestral) and exclude analogies (convergent characters). The techniques of evolutionary taxonomy are imperfect. Evolutionary biologists are aware of this and in such a situation, they prefer to classify according to phenotypic divergence.

COMPETENCY 8.0   **UNDERSTAND THE THEORY, EVIDENCE, AND MECHANISMS OF EVOLUTION**

Skill 8.1 Recognizing the historical development and mechanisms of Darwinian evolutionary theory

There are two broad theories pertaining to the rate of evolution. **Gradualism** is the theory that minor evolutionary changes occur at a regular, slow but constant, rate. Darwin's *On the Origin of Species* suggests this theory of gradualism.

Charles Darwin was born in 1809 and spent 1831 to 1836 on a ship called the *Beagle*. The *Beagle* circumnavigated the global and also called at the Galapagos Islands, a place that infatuated Darwin. There, he collected 13 species of finch that were quite similar. He could not accurately determine whether these finches were of the same species. He later learned these finches were in fact separate species. Darwin began to hypothesize that a new species arose from its ancestors by the gradual collection of adaptations to a different environmental niche. Darwin's most popular hypothesis involves the beak size of Galapagos finches. He theorized that the finches' beak sizes evolved to accommodate different food sources. Many people did not credit Darwin's theories until field studies strongly supported them.

Although Darwin thought the origin of species was gradual, he was bewildered by the gaps in the fossil records of the ancestors of living organisms. **Punctuated equilibrium** is a model of evolution that suggests that new species form rapidly over relatively short periods of geological history, and then progress through long stages of stasis with little or no change. Punctuationalists use fossil records to support their claim. It is probable that both gradualism and punctuated equilibrium are correct, depending on the particular lineage being studied.

Skill 8.2 Identifying sources of variation in a population on which natural selection can act (e.g., mutations, genetic drift)

Different molecular and environmental processes and conditions drive the evolution of populations. The various mechanisms of evolution either introduce new genetic variation or alter the frequency of existing variation.

Mutation, random changes in nucleotide sequence, is a basic mechanism of evolution. Mutations in DNA may result from copying errors during cell division, exposure to mutagens, or interaction with viruses. Simple point mutations, deletions, or insertions can alter the function or expression of existing genes but do not contribute greatly to evolutionary diversity. On the other hand, gene duplication often leads to the creation of new genes that may significantly contribute to the evolution of a species. Because gene duplication results in two copies of the same gene, the extra copy is free to mutate and develop without the selective pressure experienced by mutated single-copy genes. Gene duplication and subsequent mutation often leads to the creation of new genes. When new genes resulting from mutations lend an organism a reproductive advantage in existing environmental conditions, natural selection and adaptive evolution are the result.

Recombination is the exchange of DNA between a pair of chromosomes during meiosis. Recombination does not introduce new genes into a population, but does influence the expression of genes and the combination of traits expressed by individuals. Thus, recombination increases the genetic diversity of populations and contributes to evolution by creating new combinations of genes upon which natural selection may operate.

Isolation is the separation of populations of a single species by environmental barriers that the organisms cannot cross. Environmental change, either gradual or sudden, often results in isolation. An example of gradual isolation is the formation of a mountain range or desert between members of a species. An example of sudden isolation is the separation of two populations of a single species by a flood or earthquake. Isolation may lead to divergent evolution because the separated populations cannot reproduce together and genetic differences accumulate. In addition, because the environment of each population potentially is different, the populations adapt and evolve differently. Extended isolation can lead to speciation, the development of new species.

Sexual reproduction and selection contributes to evolution by consolidating genetic mutations and creating new combinations of genes. Genetic recombination during sexual reproduction, as previously discussed, introduces new combinations of traits and patterns of gene expression. Consolidation of favorable mutations through sexual reproduction speeds the processes of evolution and natural selection. On the other hand, consolidation of deleterious mutations creates completely unfit individuals that are readily eliminated from the population.

Genetic drift is, along with natural selection, one of the two main mechanisms of evolution. Genetic drift refers to the chance deviation in the frequency of alleles (traits) resulting from the randomness of zygote formation and selection or from chance occurrences in the environment. Because only a small percentage of all possible zygotes become mature adults, parents do not necessarily pass all of their alleles on to their offspring. Genetic drift is particularly important in small populations because chance deviations in allelic frequency can quickly alter the genotypic make-up of the population. In extreme cases, certain alleles may completely disappear from the gene pool. Genetic drift is particularly influential when environmental events and conditions produce small, isolated populations.

Skill 8.3 Analyzing the role of natural selection in leading to genotypic and phenotypic changes in a population over time

Natural selection is the term given to naturally occurring processes which favor or disfavor certain traits in a variable population over the course of generational time. The phrase "survival of the fittest" is often associated with natural selection; the fitness of an individual is measured by the contribution the individual makes to the gene pool of the next generation relative to other members of the same population.

Natural selection acts on phenotypes. An organism's phenotype is constantly exposed to its environment. Based on an organism's phenotype, selection indirectly adapts a population to its environment by maintaining favorable genotypes in the gene pool.

There are three modes of natural selection. **Stabilizing selection** favors the more common phenotypes, **directional selection** shifts the frequency of phenotypes in one direction, and **diversifying selection** favors individuals with extreme phenotypes.

Sexual selection is the term given to the favor or disfavor of certain traits by potential reproductive partners. The process of sexual selection may appear to lead to change which is not favorable for survival within the environment—for example, the brilliant plumage found in some species of birds. However, a male bird that lacks brilliant plumage may not attract females, and thus the genes for dull plumage will decrease in the population.

Skill 8.4 Demonstrating knowledge of population genetics, including factors that contribute to changing allele frequencies in a population (e.g., genetic drift, founder effect)

Population genetics is the study of a population's allele frequency, and its dispersal and change as a response to evolutionary forces. Natural selection and mutation play a role in allele frequency, and are both explained elsewhere in this manual. This section of the document focuses on genetic drift and the founder effect.

The founder effect occurs when a small number of individuals establish a new and isolated population. As such, only a small percentage of the original population's genetic variation is present, and the newly formed population may be quite different from the original. Additionally, the new and small population will experience genetic drift and demonstrate increased inbreeding. The founder is thought to be frequently responsible for the rapid creation of new species.

Genetic drift refers to the chance deviation in the frequency of alleles (traits) resulting from the randomness of zygote formation and selection or from chance occurrences in the environment. Because only a small percentage of all possible zygotes become mature adults, parents do not necessarily pass all of their alleles on to their offspring. Genetic drift is particularly important in small populations because chance deviations in allelic frequency can quickly alter the genotypic make-up of the population. In extreme cases, certain alleles may completely disappear from the gene pool.

Skill 8.5 Demonstrating knowledge of factors that contribute to speciation (e.g., geographic isolation, reproductive isolation)

In introductory biology education, the most commonly used definition of species is termed the **Biological Species Concept (BSC)**.

This concept states that a species is a reproductive community of populations that occupy a specific niche in nature. It focuses on reproductive isolation of populations as the primary criterion for recognition of species status. The biological species concept does not apply to organisms that are asexual in their reproduction, fossil organisms, or distinctive populations that hybridize.

Reproductive isolation is caused by any factor that impedes two populations from producing viable, fertile hybrids. Reproductive barriers can be categorized as **prezygotic** (premating) or **postzygotic** (postmating).

Prezygotic barriers include:

1. Habitat isolation – species occupy different habitats in the same territory
2. Temporal isolation – species reach sexual maturity at different times of the year
3. Ethological isolation – behavioral differences that reduce or prevent interbreeding between individuals of different species (including pheromones and other attractants)
4. Mechanical isolation – structural differences that make gamete transfer difficult or impossible
5. Gametic isolation – male and female gametes do not attract each other or are biochemically incompatible; no fertilization Possible

1. Postzygotic barriers include:

1. Hybrid inviability – hybrids die before sexual maturity
2. Hybrid sterility – hybrids do not form gametes or their games are not functional
3. Hybrid breakdown – hybrids may survive and reproduce, but their offspring are generally unfit

Geographical isolation can also lead to the origin of species. **Allopatric speciation** is speciation without geographic overlap. It is the accumulation of genetic differences through division of a species' range, either through a physical barrier separating the populations or through expansion by dispersal. In **sympatric speciation**, new species arise within the range of parent populations; e.g., populations are sympatric if their geographical range overlaps. This usually involves the rapid accumulation of genetic differences (usually chromosomal rearrangements) that prevent interbreeding with adjacent populations.

Skill 8.6 Analyzing evidence that species change over time (e.g., fossil record, molecular genetics)

Fossils are one key to understanding biological history. They are the preserved remnants left by an organism that lived in the past. Scientists have established the geological time scale to describe the age of fossils. The geological time scale is broken down into four eras: the Precambrian, Paleozoic, Mesozoic, and Cenozoic. The eras are further broken down into periods that represent a distinct age in the history of the Earth and its life. Scientists use rock layers called strata to date fossils. The older layers of rock usually are at the bottom. This allows scientists to correlate the rock layers with the era from which they date. Radiometric dating is a more precise method of dating fossils. Rocks and fossils contain isotopes captured during formation; over time, many of the isotopes degrade. A comparison of isotope levels between the current environment and the sample establishes the age of the sample. The isotope's half-life is used to date older fossils by determining the amount of isotope remaining and comparing it to the half-life.

Dating fossils is helpful in the construction of evolutionary trees. Scientists can arrange the succession of animals based on their fossil record. The fossils of an animal's ancestors can be dated and arranged in an evolutionary tree. For example, the branched evolution of horses shows that the modern horse's ancestors generally were smaller, had a reduced number of toes, and had teeth modified for grazing.

Molecular genetics is the study of the structure and function of genes at the molecular level. The genetic structures and sequences of an organism's DNA reveal the organism's evolutionary history. Scientists use tools of molecular genetics to study mutations in DNA that can lead to natural selection and evolution. The study of DNA using molecular genetic techniques provides us with statistics such as the 95% similarity between the DNA of humans and chimpanzees.

There are many observations and examples in molecular genetics that show evolutionary relationships between organisms. For example, the amino acid sequence of Cytochrome c, a respiratory pigment found in eukaryotic cells, has changed slowly over time. Thus, when comparing two organisms, the amount of difference between the amino acid sequence of Cytochrome c estimates the degree of evolutionary relationship. The smaller the difference, the closer the relationship between the organisms. Humans and chimpanzees have identical Cytochrome c sequences, the difference between humans and rhesus monkeys is a single amino acid, the difference between humans and penguins is 11 amino acids, and the difference between humans and yeast is 38 amino acids. Such comparisons support the evolutionary theory that small changes in DNA sequence can lead to large diversions in lineages.

Another observation in molecular genetics related to evolutionary theory is the origin of mitochondria in eukaryotic cells. Studies and comparisons of mitochondrial DNA and bacterial DNA reveal a close relationship. From these observations, many scientists hypothesize that mitochondria originated from free-living bacteria.

COMPETENCY 9.0   **UNDERSTAND REPRODUCTION, DEVELOPMENT, AND LIFE CYCLES OF LIVING ORGANISMS**

Skill 9.1 Demonstrating knowledge of the characteristics of sexual and asexual reproduction, including advantages and disadvantages of each

The obvious advantage of asexual reproduction is that it does not require a partner. This is a huge advantage for sessile organisms such as the hydra. Not having to move around to reproduce also allows organisms to conserve energy. Asexual reproduction also tends to be faster. There are disadvantages, as in the case of regeneration in plants. If the plant is not in good condition or in the case of spore-producing plants, if the surrounding conditions are not suitable for the spores to grow the plant's asexual offspring likely will have trouble surviving.

In addition, as asexual reproduction produces only exact genetic copies of the parent organism, it does not allow for genetic variation, which means that deleterious mutations, or weaker qualities, will always be passed on. This can also be detrimental to a species well adapted to a particular environment when the conditions of that environment change suddenly. On the whole, however, asexual reproduction is more reliable because it requires fewer steps and is less error-prone.

Sexual reproduction combines genetic information from gametes produced by genetically distinct parents, thereby producing new genetic variety in the species. This can result in a better species with an improved chance of long-term survival. There is, however, the disadvantage that sexual reproduction requires a partner, which in turn may require locating a mate, courtship, and copulation.

Skill 9.2 Recognizing processes related to developing embryos (e.g., cleavage, gastrulation, organogenesis)

Development is defined as a change in form. Most animals go through several stages of development after fertilization of the egg cell, including initial cleavage, the blastula phase, gastrulation, neuralation, and organogenesis.

> **Cleavage** - the first divisions of the fertilized egg
> **Blastula** - a hollow ball of undifferentiated cells
> **Gastrulation** - the time of tissue differentiation into the separate germ layers, the endoderm, mesoderm, and ectoderm
> **Neuralation** - development of the nervous system
> **Organogenesis** - the development of the various organs of the body

Embryonic induction is the process in which developing embryonic tissue influences surrounding tissue, thus changing the responding tissue's pattern of differentiation. For example, the development of neural tissue in a developing embryo relies on embryonic induction. Some ectodermal cells develop into neuroectoderm, the precursor of the nervous system, when signaled by tissue in the notochord, the central axis of the embryo. Embryonic induction is comparable to hormonal activity in adult animals. Hormones released by cells often stimulate growth and development of other cells.

Studying ontogeny, the origin and development of an organism from fertilization to adulthood, provides insight into the evolutionary history of an organism. In fact, some scientists in the 19th century mistakenly believed ontogeny recapitulated phylogeny—in other words, an organism's evolutionary development was preserved, step-by-step in the development of the embryo. While this theory has been discredited, some ancestral characteristics do appear in the developmental stages of embryos. For example, both chicken and human embryos pass through a stage where they have pharyngeal slits that are similar to the gill slits of fish. In addition, human embryos possess tail-like structures at one point in their development. The appearance of such traits helps link species to their evolutionary ancestors.

Skill 9.3 Analyzing factors (e.g., genetics, nutrition, disease) that impact the growth and development of organisms

There are many factors that influence an organism's development and tissue differentiation. Even when fully formed and mature, organisms continue to grow and change. Below are several important factors:

Genetics
Genetic composition is perhaps the single most important factor in determining the growth and development of an individual organism. Genes code for the proteins that determine all the traits of a creature. Though other factors have an influence, the genes provide the road map for the differentiation of tissues and the development of the organism.

Hormones and growth factors
These molecules trigger the growth and differentiation of cells during an embryo's development, the growth of organs and tissues, and an individual's maturation. It is critical that they be present in the correct place, at the correct time, and in the correct concentration. Thus, if there are errors in their production, important pre-cursors are absent, or they (or similar molecules) are introduced artificially, the individual's development will be altered.

Nutrition

Access to the proper nutrients, including food, water and select inorganic compounds, is important for all organisms. These items provide important precursors for synthesis reactions and the energy for metabolic activities. Lack of nutrients is particularly likely to retard the growth of organisms.

Gravity

This factor is especially important to the development of plants, which rely on gravity to trigger the downward growth of roots and upward growth of stems. Gravity is also thought to be an important factor in the development and maintenance of the muscular and skeletal systems in animals.

Sunlight

Like gravity, sunlight is especially important to the growth of plants, since they rely on it to manufacture the energy they require for all functions. Not only is it important to their development, mature plants will bend toward sunlight to maximize their exposure. Access to sunlight is also important to animals, many of which need it to synthesize important nutrients (e.g., vitamin D).

Disease and parasites

There are a very wide range of diseases and parasites that can disrupt growth and development through a variety of mechanisms. The deleterious impact of parasites may be as simple as diverting resources from the organism's essential functions, thus retarding growth. Diseases may also alter the operation of certain tissues or organs, thereby disturbing various processes of the individual. This in turn can alter growth patterns or upset development.

Pollutants, drugs, and other artificial chemicals

Much like diseases, pollutants and other chemicals can interfere with or imitate growth factors and enzymes. They can also disrupt important signaling pathways or destroy cells and tissues. Thus, these substances can be extremely damaging. Moreover, if exposure to these compounds occurs during development, they can prevent the proper differentiation of cells and deform or kill the organism.

Skill 9.4 Demonstrating knowledge of the life cycles of prokaryotes, plants, animals, and fungi

Single-Celled Organisms

Bacteria reproduce by binary fission. This asexual process is simply dividing the bacterium in half. All new organisms are genetic clones of the parent.

Some bacteria have a sticky capsule that protects the cell wall and is also used for adhesion to surfaces. Pili are surface appendages for adhesion to other cells.

A **plasmid** is a small ring of DNA that carries accessory genes separate from those of a bacterial chromosome. Most plasmids in Gram-negative bacteria undergo bidirectional replication, although some replicate unidirectionally because of their small size. Plasmids in Gram-positive bacteria replicate by the rolling circle mechanism.

Some plasmids can transfer themselves (and therefore their genetic information) by a process called conjugation. Conjugation requires cell-to-cell contact. The sex pilus of the donor cell attaches to the recipient cell. Once contact has been established, the transfer of DNA occurs by the rolling circle mechanism.

Protists are thought to be the earliest eukaryotic descendants of prokaryotes. Protists are found almost anywhere there is water. Protists can be broadly defined as eukaryotic microorganisms and include the macroscopic algae with only a single tissue type. They are defined by exclusion of characteristics common of the other eukaryotic kingdoms. They are not prokaryotes because they usually have a true nucleus and membrane-bound organelles. They are not fungi because fungi lack undulopidia and develop from spores. They are not plants because plants develop from embryos, and they are not animals because animals develop from a blastula.

Plants

Plants accomplish reproduction through alternation of generations. Simply stated, a haploid stage in the plants life history alternates with a diploid stage. The diploid sporophyte divides by meiosis to reduce the chromosome number as appropriate for the haploid gametophyte generation. The haploid gametophytes undergo mitosis to produce gametes (sperm and eggs). Finally, the haploid gametes fertilize to return to the correct chromosome count for the diploid sporophyte stage.

Non-vascular plants need water to reproduce. The vascular, non-seeded plants reproduce with spores and also need water to reproduce. Gymnosperms use seeds for reproduction and do not require water. Angiosperms are the most numerous and are therefore the main focus of reproduction in the remainder of this section.

In a process called **pollination**, plant anthers release pollen grains and animals and the wind carry the grains to plant carpels.

The sperm are released from the pollen grain to fertilize the eggs. Angiosperms reproduce through a method of double fertilization. Two sperm fertilize an ovum. One sperm produces the new plant and the other forms the food supply for the developing plant (endosperm). The ovule develops into a seed and the ovary develops into a fruit. Then the wind or animals carry the seeds to new locations in a process called **dispersal**.

The development of the egg to form a plant occurs in three stages: growth, morphogenesis (the development of form) and cellular differentiation (the acquisition of a cell's specific structure and function).

<u>Humans</u>
Hormones regulate sexual maturation in humans. Humans cannot reproduce until about the puberty age of 8-14, depending on the individual. The hypothalamus begins secreting hormones that stimulate maturation of the reproductive system and development of the secondary sex characteristics. Reproductive maturity in females occurs with the first menstruation and occurs in males with the first ejaculation of viable sperm.

Hormones also regulate reproduction. In males, the primary sex hormones are the androgens, testosterone being the most important. The androgens are produced in the testes and are responsible for the primary and secondary sex characteristics of the male. Female hormone patterns are cyclic and complex. Most females have a reproductive cycle length of about 28 days. The menstrual cycle corresponds to changes in the uterus. The ovarian cycle results in ovulation and occurs in parallel with the menstrual cycle. This parallelism is regulated by hormones. Five hormones participate in this regulation, most notably estrogen and progesterone. Estrogen and progesterone play an important role in the signaling to the uterus and the development and maintenance of the endometruim. Estrogens are also responsible for the secondary sex characteristics of females.

Gametogenesis is the production of the sperm and egg cells.

Spermatogenesis begins at puberty in the male. One spermatogonia, the diploid precursor of haploid sperm, produces four sperm. The sperm mature in the seminiferous tubules located in the testes. **Oogenesis**, the production of haploid egg cells (ova), is usually complete by the birth of a female. Egg cells are not released until menstruation begins at puberty. Meiosis forms one haploid ovum with a large amount of cytoplasm and three polar bodies that are reabsorbed by the body. The ovum are stored in the ovaries and released each month from puberty to menopause.

Sperm are stored in the seminiferous tubules in the testes where they mature. Mature sperm are found in the epididymis located on top of the testes. During ejaculation, the sperm travel up the **vas deferens** where they mix with semen made in the prostate and seminal vesicles and travel out the urethra.

Ovulation releases the egg into the fallopian tubes that are ciliated to move the egg along. Fertilization of the egg by the sperm normally occurs in the fallopian tube. If pregnancy does not occur, the egg passes through the uterus and is expelled through the vagina during menstruation. Levels of progesterone and estrogen stimulate menstruation and are controlled by the implantation of a fertilized egg so menstruation will not occur.

If fertilization occurs, the zygote begins dividing about 24 hours later. The resulting cells form a blastocyst that implants in the uterus about two to three days later. Implantation promotes secretion of human chorionic gonadotrophin (HCG). This is what is detected in pregnancy tests. The HCG keeps the level of progesterone elevated to maintain the uterine lining in order to feed the developing embryo until the umbilical cord forms.

Organogenesis, the development of the body organs, occurs during the first trimester of fetal development. The heart begins to beat and all the major structures are present at this time. The fetus grows very rapidly during the second trimester of pregnancy. The fetus is about 30 cm long and is very active at this stage. During the final third trimester, fetal activity may decrease as the fetus grows. Labor is initiated by oxytocin, which causes labor contractions and dilation of the cervix. Prolactin and oxytocin cause the production of milk.

COMPETENCY 10.0   UNDERSTAND THE STRUCTURES, ORGANIZATION, AND FUNCTIONS OF SYSTEMS IN ORGANISMS

Skill 10.1   Demonstrating knowledge of the anatomical structures, organ systems, and physiological processes (e.g., digestion, excretion, transpiration) that allow organisms to carry out specific life functions

Members of the five different kingdoms of the classification system of living organisms often differ in their basic life functions. Here we compare and analyze how members of the five kingdoms obtain nutrients, excrete waste, and reproduce.

Bacteria are prokaryotic, single-celled organisms that lack cell nuclei. The different types of bacteria obtain nutrients in a variety of ways. Chemotophs absorb nutrients from the environment through small channels in their cell walls and membranes,while phototrophs perform photosynthesis. Chemoorganotrophs use organic compounds as energy sources, while chemolithotrophs use both organic and inorganic chemicals as energy sources. Depending on the type of metabolism and energy source, bacteria release a variety of waste products (e.g., alcohols, acids, carbon dioxide) to the environment through diffusion.

All bacteria reproduce through binary fission (asexual reproduction) producing two genetically identical cells. Bacteria reproduce very rapidly, with some types dividing every twenty minutes in optimal conditions. Asexual reproduction does not allow for as much genetic variability as sexual reproduction, but bacteria achieve genetic variety by absorbing DNA from ruptured cells and conjugating or swapping chromosomal or plasmid DNA with other cells.

Animals are multicellular, eukaryotic organisms. All animals obtain nutrients by eating food (ingestion). Different types of animals derive nutrients from eating plants, other animals, or both. Animal cells perform respiration that converts food molecules, mainly carbohydrates and fats, into energy. The excretory systems of animals, like animals themselves, vary in complexity. Simple invertebrates eliminate waste through a single tube, while complex vertebrates have a specialized system of organs that process and excrete waste.

Most animals, unlike bacteria, exist in two distinct sexes. Members of the female sex give live birth or lay eggs. Some less developed animals can reproduce asexually. For example, flatworms can divide in two and some unfertilized insect eggs can develop into viable organisms. Most animals reproduce sexually through various mechanisms. For example, aquatic animals reproduce by external fertilization of eggs, while mammals reproduce by internal fertilization. More complex animals possess specialized reproductive systems and cycles that facilitate reproduction and promote genetic variation.

Plants, like animals, are multicellular, eukaryotic organisms. Most plants obtain nutrients from the soil through their root systems and convert sunlight into energy through photosynthesis. Many plants store waste products in vacuoles or structures (e.g. leaves, bark) that are discarded. Some plants also excrete waste through their roots. Plants expel water through their leaf stomata in a process called transpiration.

More than half of all of the world's plant species reproduce by producing seeds from which new plants grow. Depending on the type of plant, flowers or cones produce seeds. Other plants reproduce by spores, tubers, bulbs, buds, and grafts. The flowers of flowering plants contain the reproductive organs. Pollination is the joining of male and female gametes—a process often facilitated by gamete movement by wind or animals.

Fungi are eukaryotic, mostly multicellular organisms. All fungi are heterotrophs, obtaining nutrients from other organisms. More specifically, most fungi obtain nutrients by digesting and absorbing nutrients from dead organisms. Fungi secrete enzymes outside of their body to digest organic material and then absorb the nutrients through their cell walls.

Most fungi can reproduce asexually and sexually. Different types of fungi reproduce asexually by mitosis, budding, sporification, or fragmentation. Sexual reproduction of fungi is different from sexual reproduction of animals. The two mating types of fungi are termed plus and minus, not male and female. The fusion of hyphae, the specialized reproductive structure in fungi, between plus and minus types produces and scatters diverse spores.

Protists are eukaryotic, single-celled organisms. Most protists are heterotrophic, obtaining nutrients by ingesting small molecules and cells and digesting them in vacuoles. All protists reproduce asexually by either binary or multiple fission. Like bacteria, protists achieve genetic variation by exchange of DNA through conjugation.

Skill 10.2 Recognizing levels of biological organization (i.e., tissues, organs, and organ systems) in multicellular organisms

Life is highly organized. The organization of living systems spans multiple levels, from small to increasingly larger and complex. Life is organized from simple to complex in the following way:

Atoms →
    Molecules →
        Organelles →
            Cells →
                Tissues →
                    Organs →
                        Organ systems →
                        Organism

Skill 10.3 Analyzing characteristics, functions, and relationships of systems in animals

Organ systems are groups of related organs. Organ systems consist of organs working together to perform a common function. The commonly recognized organ systems of e.g. mammals include the reproductive system, nervous system, circulatory system, respiratory system, lymphatic system (immune system), endocrine system, urinary system, muscular system, digestive system, integumentary system, and skeletal system. In addition, organ systems are interconnected, as a single system rarely works alone to complete a task.

One obvious example of the interconnectedness of organ systems is the relationship between the circulatory and respiratory systems. As blood circulates through the organs of the circulatory systems, it is re-oxygenated in the lungs of the respiratory system. Another example is the influence of the endocrine system on other organ systems. Hormones released by the endocrine system greatly influence processes of many organ systems including the nervous and reproductive systems.

In addition, bodily response to infection is a coordinated effort of the lymphatic (immune) system and circulatory systems. The lymphatic system produces specialized immune cells, filters out disease-causing organisms, and removes fluid waste from in and around tissue. The lymphatic system utilizes capillary structures of the circulatory system and interacts with blood cells in a coordinated response to infection.

The muscular and skeletal systems are closely related. Skeletal muscles attach to the bones of the skeleton and drive movement of the body.

Animal tissue becomes specialized during development. The ectoderm (outer layer) becomes the epidermis or skin. The mesoderm (middle layer) becomes muscles and other organs beside the gut. The endoderm (inner layer) becomes the gut, also called the archenteron.

Animals constantly require oxygen for cellular respiration and need to eliminate carbon dioxide from their bodies. For air-breathing animals, the respiratory surface must be large and moist. Different animal groups have different types of respiratory organs to perform gas exchange. Some animals use their entire outer skin for respiration (as in the case of worms). Fishes and other aquatic animals have gills for gas exchange. Ventilation increases the flow of water over the gills. This process brings oxygen and removes carbon dioxide through the gills. Fish use a large amount of energy to ventilate their gills. This is because the oxygen available in water is less than that available in the air and because water is more dense than air and is thus more difficult to move. The arthropoda (insects) have tracheal tubes that send air to all parts of their bodies. Gas exchange for smaller insects is provided by diffusion. Larger insects ventilate their bodies by a series of body movements that compress and expand the tracheal tubes. Air-breathing vertebrates have lungs as their primary respiratory organ. The gas exchange system in most vertebrates is similar to the system used by humans, discussed in a later section.

Osmoregulation and excretion in many invertebrates involves tubular systems that branch throughout the body. Interstitial fluid enters these tubes and is collected into excretory ducts that empty into the external environment by openings in the body wall. Insects have excretory organs called Malpighian tubules. These organs pump water, salts, and nitrogenous wastes into the tubules. These fluids then pass through the hindgut and out the rectum. Vertebrates have kidneys as the primary excretion organ. This system is described in a later section.

Skill 10.4 Analyzing characteristics, functions, and relationships of systems in plants

Plants require adaptations that allow them to absorb light for photosynthesis. Since they are unable to move about, they must evolve methods to allow them to reproduce successfully. Over evolutionary history, plants moved from a water environment onto the land. Advantages of life on land include more available light and a higher concentration of carbon dioxide. Originally, there were no predators and less competition for space on land. Plants had to evolve methods of support, reproduction, respiration, and conservation of water once they moved to land. Reproduction by plants is accomplished through alternation of generations. Simply stated, a haploid stage in the plant species' life history alternates with a diploid stage. A division of labor among plant tissues evolved in order to obtain water and minerals from the earth. A wax cuticle is produced on the leaves to prevent the loss of water. Leaves enabled plants to capture light and carbon dioxide for photosynthesis. Stomata provide openings on the underside of leaves for oxygen to diffuse in or out of the plant and for carbon dioxide to diffuse in. A method of anchorage (roots) evolved. The polymer lignin evolved to give tremendous strength to plants.

Roots, stems, leaves, and reproductive structures are the most functionally important parts of plant anatomy. Different types of plants have distinctive anatomical structures. Thus, a discussion of plant anatomy requires an understanding of the classifications of plants.

Roots absorb water and minerals and exchange gases in the soil. Like stems, roots contain xylem and phloem. The xylem transports water and minerals, called xylem sap, upwards. The sugar produced by photosynthesis goes down the phloem in the phloem sap, traveling to the roots and other non-photosynthetic parts of the plant. In addition to water and mineral absorption, roots anchor plants in place preventing erosion by environmental conditions.

Stems are the major support structure of plants. Stems consist primarily of three types of tissue, namely dermal tissue, ground tissue, and vascular tissue. Dermal tissue covers the outside surface of the stem to prevent excessive water loss and control gas exchange. Ground tissue consists mainly of parenchyma cells and surrounds the vascular tissue providing support and protection. Finally, vascular tissues, xylem and phloem, provide long distance transport of nutrients and water.

Leaves enable plants to capture light and carbon dioxide for photosynthesis, which occurs primarily in the leaves. Plants exchange gases through small openings on the undersides of their leaves, called stomata. Stomata allow oxygen to diffuse in or out of the plant and carbon dioxide to diffuse in. Leaf size and shape varies greatly between species of plants and botanists often identify plants by their characteristic leaf patterns.

Reproductive Structures

The sporophyte is the dominant phase in plant reproduction. Sporophytes contain a diploid set of chromosomes and form haploid spores by meiosis. Spores develop into gametophytes that produce gametes by mitosis. Angiosperm reproductive structures are flowers.

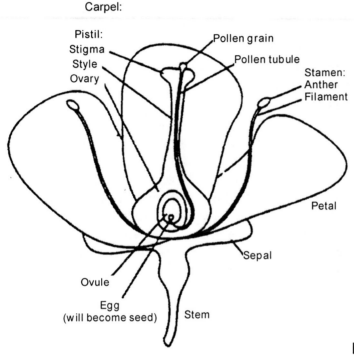

Figure 15

The male gametophytes are pollen grains and the female gametophytes are embryo sacs that are inside of the ovules. The male pollen grains form in the anthers at the tips of the stamens. The ovaries contain the female ovules. Finally, the stamen is the reproductive organ of the male and the carpel is the reproductive organ of the female. Often, a single flower will have both male and female reproductive organs.

The **non-vascular plants** represent a grade of evolution characterized by several primitive features for plants: lack of roots, lack of conducting tissues, reliance on absorption of water that falls on the plant or condenses on the plant in high humidity, and a lack of leaves. Non-vascular plants include the liverworts, hornworts, and mosses. Each is recognized as a separate division.

The characteristics of **vascular plants** are as follows: synthesis of lignin to give rigidity and strength to cell walls for growing upright; evolution of tracheid cells for water transport and sieve cells for nutrient transport; and the use of underground stems (rhizomes) as a structure from which adventitious roots originate.

There are two kinds of vascular plants: non-seeded and seeded. The non-seeded vascular plant divisions include Division Lycophyta (club moses), Division Sphenophyta (horsetails), and Division Pterophyta (ferns). The seeded vascular plants differ from the non-seeded plants in method of reproduction, which will be discussed later. The vascular seed plants are divided into two groups, the gymnosperms and the angiosperms.

Gymnosperms were the first plants to evolve with the use of seeds for reproduction, which made them less dependent on water to assist in reproduction. Their pollen is carried by the wind. Gymnosperms have cones that protect the seeds. Gymnosperm divisions include Division Cycadophyta (cycads), Division Ginkgophyta (ginkgo), Division Gnetophyta (gnetophytes), and Division Coniferophyta (conifers).

Angiosperms are the largest division in the plant kingdom. They are the flowering plants and produce true seeds for reproduction. They arose about seventy million years ago when the dinosaurs were disappearing. The land was drying up and the ability to produce seeds that could remain dormant until conditions became acceptable allowed for angiosperm success. They also have more advanced vascular tissue and larger leaves for increased photosynthesis. Angiosperms consist of only one division, the Anthrophyta. Angiosperms are divided into monocots and dicots. Monocots have one cotelydon (seed leaf) and parallel veins on their leaves. Their flower petals are in multiples of threes. Dicots have two cotelydons and branching veins on their leaves. Flower petals are in multiples of fours or fives.

COMPETENCY 11.0   UNDERSTAND HOW ORGANISMS OBTAIN, STORE, AND USE MATTER AND ENERGY

Skill 11.1 Demonstrating knowledge of processes used by organisms (i.e., heterotrophs and autotrophs) to obtain energy

An **autotroph** (self-eater) is an organism that make its own food from the energy of the sun or chemical compounds. Autotrophs include:

1. **photoautotrophs** - make food from light and carbon dioxide, and release oxygen that can be used for respiration; plants, some protists, and some bacteria are photoautotrophs
2. **chemoautotrophs** - oxidize sulfur and ammonia compounds; some bacteria are chemoautotrophs.

Heterotrophs (other eater) are organisms that must eat other organisms or energy-rich organic compounds to obtain energy. Another term for heterotroph is **consumer**. All animals are heterotrophs. **Decomposers** break down once living things. Bacteria and fungi are examples of decomposers. **Scavengers** eat dead things. Examples of scavengers are bacteria, fungi, and some animals.

Skill 11.2 Demonstrating knowledge of ways in which animals obtain food and water

In order to survive, organisms must be able to satisfy several basic needs. They must be able to obtain energy and avoid being used as energy, obtain and conserve water, and find a space in which they can survive the extremes of abiotic factors.

Organisms obtain food in a variety of methods depending largely on the organism and the environment. Some single-celled organisms obtain food by crawling toward prey, engulfing it, and digesting it internally, while others make their own food by using energy from the sun in the same manner that plants do. The food web demonstrates how animals obtain food, having to catch and digest prey in order to obtain the nutrients and energy to survive. It is important to recognize that the only manner for most heterotrophs to obtain food is by taking the energy from another organism.

Organisms obtain water either from a water source, or from the digestion of other organisms in the same manner they obtain food. Organisms may obtain water from pools of water, lakes, streams, rivers, and oceans. Other organisms, which cannot obtain water from a water source, must attempt to obtain sufficient water from the food that they consume.

Skill 11.3 Demonstrating knowledge of ways in which plants obtain nutrients and water

Plants are autotrophs. Plants are able to obtain their food using the sun's light through the process of photosynthesis (see section 3.2). Vascular plants rely on the soil for most of the water they absorb. Plants are perfectly suited for their lifestyle. The tissue structure of plants is as follows:

Ground tissue occupies the space between the dermal and vascular tissue and synthesizes organic compounds, supports the plant, and provides storage for the plant. Ground tissue consists of parenchyma, sclerenchyma, and collenchyma tissue. Parenchyma is the main component of ground tissue and is the progenitor of all other tissue. Parenchyma cells are living at maturity, non-specialized, and perform most of the plant metabolic activities. Sclerenchyma tissue consists of non-living cells that are very rigid and have secondary walls and a hardening agent that provide support to the plant. Finally, collenchyma tissue consists of living cells that are somewhat rigid and provide support to growing plants, but do not possess secondary walls or a hardening agent.

Dermal tissue is the outermost layer of plant leaves, stems, fruits, seeds, and roots. Dermal tissue interacts with the environment and its functions include gas exchange, light passage, and pathogen recognition. One subtype of dermal tissue is the epidermis. The epidermis is usually a single layer of unspecialized cells, either parenchyma or sclerenchyma. In plants that undergo secondary growth, another subtype of dermal tissue called periderm replaces the epidermis on the stems and roots. Periderm, also called bark, consists of parenchyma, sclerenchyma, and cork cells. The function of the periderm is to prevent excess water loss, protect against pathogens, and provide insulation to the plant.

Vascular tissue consists of xylem and phloem and facilitates the transport of water and nutrients throughout the plant. Xylem is a sclerenchyma tissue that conducts water and transports minerals from the soil up the plant. The two types of conductive cells in the xylem are tracheids and vessels. Vessels are much larger in diameter and serve as the major pipes in the water transport system of the plant. Phloem is a parenchyma tissue that functions in the transport of sugars, amino acids, and other small molecules from the leaves to the rest of the plant. The two types of specialized cells in the phloem are sieve elements and companion cells. Sieve elements possess thin cell walls and pores that facilitate transfer of nutrients. Companion cells accompany sieve element cells and help maintain the life functions of the sieve cells.

Skill 11.4 Demonstrating knowledge of strategies used by organisms to store nutrients

Vacuoles are one of the most common storage compartments used by simple organisms and plants. Though we commonly think of vacuoles as simply the organelle employed by plant cells to maintain turgor pressure, they actually have a variety of functions. For example, in budding yeast cells, vacuoles are used as storage compartments for amino acids. When the yeast cells are deprived of food, proteins stored in the vacuoles are consumed. This process is known as autophagy. Additionally, protists and macrophages use vacuoles to hold food when they engage in phagocytosis (the cellular intake of large molecules or other cells).

Plants have evolved various methods to store excess food. While some store extra glucose, many plants store starch in their roots and stems. Seeds are often "packaged" with additional stored food in the form of both sugar and starch. Many common examples of such plant "storage devices" are exploited as food by humans. For instance, carrots are large roots packed with the plant's extra food. Most fruits, nuts, and edible seeds also contain many calories intended to nurture the next generation of plants.

In many animals, adipose (fat) tissue is used to store extra metabolic energy for long periods. The liver metabolizes excess calories into fat. Adipocytes store this synthesized fat and dietary fat. When the body needs energy, it can break down the stored fat supply to use fatty acids and glycerol in metabolism. The body can convert glycerol to glucose and many cells in the body can use it as a source of energy, while the heart and skeletal muscle especially need fatty acids. The storage and use of this fat is under the control of several hormones including insulin, glucagons, and epinephrine.

Skill 11.5 Analyzing processes by which nutrients are obtained and distributed to all parts of an organism

Complex, multicellular organisms must have systems to distribute nutrients to all their various tissues. The following describes these systems in plants and animals.

Plants

Most of the large, complex plants are termed vascular plants because they possess specialized tissues to transport water. Vascular plants include ferns, club mosses, horsetails, all flowering plants, conifers, and gymnosperms. Plants synthesize glucose through photosynthesis in their leaves and obtain water and certain nutrients (nitrogen, phosphorus) through their roots. The vascular system in plants consists of xylem and phloem. The xylem carries water and inorganic solutes up from the roots, while the phloem carries the organic solutes (mostly sugars) from the leaves to the rest of the plant.

Note that there are certain simple plants, such as mosses, liverworts, and hornworts, that are nonvascular. These plants must rely on diffusion alone to distribute water and nutrients. Therefore, the size to which these plants may grow is limited.

Animals

The circulatory system in animals is the equivalent of the vascular system in plants. The very simplest animals do not have a circulatory system. Flatworms, for instance, lack circulatory systems. Their mouths lead directly to highly branched digestive systems. Nutrients, water, and gas simply diffuse from the digestive system into all the cells in the flatworm. Relying on diffusion alone to transport nutrients necessarily limits the size and complexity of organisms.

The circulatory system in any animal serves to deliver gases (oxygen) as well as nutrients from the digestive system to all the tissues of the body.

Certain animals, including mollusks and arthropods, possess open circulatory systems. The circulatory fluid, called hemolymph, in these animals is rather like a combination of the blood and interstitial fluid present in higher species. The heart pumps the hemolymph into a fairly large, open cavity called the hemocoel. In the hemocoel, the hemolymph directly bathes all the animal's tissues and delivers nutrients. The hemolymph is composed of water, electrolytes, and organic compounds (i.e., carbohydrates, proteins, etc).

Higher species have closed circulatory systems, consisting of arteries, capillaries, and veins that confine the blood. In these systems, the blood passes through tiny capillaries in the lungs and small intestines and absorbs oxygen and nutrients, respectively. The blood is pumped to all the tissues of the body, where the oxygen and nutrients diffuse through the walls of more tiny capillaries. In general, arteries take oxygen and nutrients to the tissues, while veins return the blood to the heart. Various species have developed closed circulatory systems of varying complexity. Fish, for example have only a two-chambered heart, while amphibians have three-chambered hearts. Birds and mammals have four-chambered hearts, allowing complete separation between blood being pumped to and from the body and blood pumped to and from the lungs.

COMPETENCY 12.0 **UNDERSTAND THE STRUCTURE AND FUNCTION OF THE HUMAN BODY**

Skill 12.1 Demonstrating knowledge of the structures and processes of the human body

Skeletal System - The skeletal system functions in body support. Vertebrates have an endoskeleton, with muscles attached to bones. Skeletal proportions are controlled by area to volume relationships. Body size and shape is limited by the forces of gravity. The axial skeleton consists of the bones of the skull and vertebrae. The appendicular skeleton consists of the bones of the legs, arms, tail, and shoulder girdle. Bone is a connective tissue.

Parts of the bone include compact bone which gives strength, spongy bone which contains red marrow to make blood cells, yellow marrow in the center of long bones to store fat cells, and the periosteum, which is the protective covering on the outside of the bone.

In addition to bones and muscles, ligaments and tendons are important joint components. A joint is a place where two bones meet. Joints enable movement. Ligaments attach bone to bone. Tendons attach bone to muscle. There are three types of joints:

1. Ball and socket – allow for rotational movement. An example is the joint between the shoulder and the humerus. This type of joint allows humans to move their arms and legs in many different ways.
2. Hinge – movement is restricted to a single plane. An example is the joint between the humerus and the ulna.
3. Pivot – allows for the rotation of the forearm at the elbow and the hands at the wrist.

Muscular System – The function of the muscular system is movement. There are three types of muscle tissue: skeletal, smooth, and cardiac. Skeletal muscle is voluntary, and attaches to bones. Smooth muscle is involuntary, is found in organs, and enables functions such as digestion and respiration. Cardiac muscle is a specialized type of smooth muscle.

Skeletal muscle is voluntary. These muscles are attached to bones and are responsible for movement. Skeletal muscle consists of long fibers and is striated due to the repeating patterns of the myofilaments (made of the proteins actin and myosin) that make up the fibers.

Cardiac muscle is found in the heart. Cardiac muscle is striated like skeletal muscle, but differs in that the plasma membrane of the cardiac muscle causes the muscle to beat even when away from the heart. The action potentials of cardiac and skeletal muscles also differ.

Smooth muscle is involuntary. It is found in organs and enables functions such as digestion and respiration. Unlike skeletal and cardiac muscle, smooth muscle is not striated. Smooth muscle has less myosin and does not generate as much tension as the striated muscles.

The mechanism of skeletal muscle contraction involves a nerve impulse striking a muscle fiber. This causes calcium ions to flood the sarcomere. The myosin fibers creep along the actin, causing the muscle to contract. Once the nerve impulse has passed, calcium is pumped out and the contraction ends.

Nervous System - The **neuron** is the basic unit of the nervous system. It consists of an axon, which carries impulses away from the cell body; dendrites, which carry impulses toward the cell body; and the cell body, which contains the nucleus. Synapses are spaces between neurons. Chemicals called neurotransmitters are found close to the synapse. The myelin sheath, composed of Schwann cells, covers the neurons and provides insulation.

Physiology of the nerve impulse - Nerve action depends on depolarization and an imbalance of electrical charges across the neuron's membrane. A polarized nerve has a positive charge outside the neuron. A depolarized nerve has a negative charge outside the neuron. Neurotransmitters turn off the sodium pump, which results in depolarization of the membrane. This wave of depolarization (as it moves from neuron to neuron) carries an electrical impulse. This is actually a wave of opening and closing gates that allows for the flow of ions across the synapse. Nerves have an action potential. There is a threshold of the level of chemicals that must be met or exceeded in order for muscles to respond. This is called the "all or none" response.

The **reflex arc** is the simplest nerve response that bypasses the brain. When a stimulus (like touching a hot stove) occurs, sensors in the hand send the message directly to the spinal cord. This stimulates motor neurons that contract the muscles to move the hand.

Voluntary nerve responses involve the brain. Receptor cells send the message to sensory neurons, which lead to association neurons. Motor neurons are stimulated and the message is transmitted to effector cells, which cause the end effect.

Organization of the Nervous System - The somatic nervous system is controlled consciously. It consists of the central nervous system (brain and spinal cord) and the peripheral nervous system (nerves that extend from the spinal cord to the muscles). The autonomic nervous system is unconsciously controlled by the hypothalamus of the brain. Smooth muscles, the heart, and digestion are some processes controlled by the autonomic nervous system. The sympathetic nervous system works generally in opposition to the parasympathetic nervous system. For example, if the sympathetic nervous system stimulates an action, the parasympathetic nervous system would end that action.

Neurotransmitters - these are chemicals released by exocytosis. Some neurotransmitters stimulate action, others inhibit action.

Acetylcholine - the most common neurotransmitter; it controls muscle contraction and heartbeat. The enzyme acetylcholinesterase breaks it down to end the transmission.

Epinephrine - responsible for the "fight or flight" reaction. It causes an increase in heart rate and blood flow to prepare the body for action. It is also called adrenaline.

Endorphins and enkephalins - these are natural pain-killers and are released during serious injury and childbirth.

Digestive System - The function of the digestive system is to break food down into nutrients and absorb nutrients into the blood stream where they can be delivered to all cells of the body for use in cellular respiration. The teeth and saliva begin digestion by breaking food down into smaller pieces and lubricating it so it can be swallowed. The lips, cheeks, and tongue form a bolus or ball of food. It is carried down the pharynx by the process of peristalsis (wave-like contractions) and enters the stomach through the sphincter, which closes to keep food from going back up. In the stomach, pepsinogen and hydrochloric acid form pepsin, the enzyme that hydrolyzes proteins. The food is broken down further by this chemical action and is churned into acid chyme. The pyloric sphincter muscle opens to allow the food to enter the small intestine.

Most nutrient absorption occurs in the small intestine. Its large surface area, accomplished by its length and protrusions called villi and microvilli, allow for a great absorptive surface into the bloodstream. Chyme is neutralized after coming from the acidic stomach to allow the enzymes found there to function. Accessory organs function in the production of necessary enzymes and bile. The pancreas makes many enzymes further to break down nutrients in the small intestine. The liver makes bile, which breaks down and emulsifies fatty acids. Any food left after the trip through the small intestine enters the large intestine. The large intestine functions to reabsorb water and produce vitamin K. The feces, or remaining waste, are passed out through the anus.

Accessory organs - although not part of the digestive tract, these organs function in the production of necessary enzymes and bile. The pancreas makes many enzymes to break down nutrients in the small intestine. The liver makes bile, which breaks down and emulsifies fatty acids.

Respiratory System - The respiratory system functions in the gas exchange of oxygen and carbon dioxide waste. It delivers oxygen to the bloodstream and picks up carbon dioxide for release out of the body. Air enters the mouth and nose, where it is warmed, moistened, and filtered of dust and particles. Cilia in the trachea trap unwanted material in mucus, which can be expelled. The trachea splits into two bronchial tubes and the bronchial tubes divide into smaller and smaller bronchioles in the lungs. The internal surface of the lung is composed of alveoli, which are thin walled air sacs. These allow for a large surface area for gas exchange. The alveoli are lined with capillaries. Oxygen diffuses into the bloodstream and carbon dioxide diffuses out of the capillaries to be exhaled out of the lungs. The oxygenated blood is carried to the heart and delivered to all parts of the body.

The thoracic cavity holds the lungs. A muscle complex, the diaphragm, below the lungs is an adaptation that makes inhalation possible. As the volume of the thoracic cavity increases, the diaphragm muscle flattens out and inhalation occurs. When the diaphragm relaxes, exhalation occurs.

Circulatory System

The function of the closed circulatory system (**cardiovascular system**) is to carry oxygenated blood and nutrients to all cells of the body and return carbon dioxide waste to be expelled from the lungs. The heart, blood vessels, and blood make up the cardiovascular system.

Be familiar with the parts of the heart and the path blood takes from the heart to the lungs, through the body and back to the heart. In short, unoxygenated blood enters the heart through the inferior and superior vena cava. The first chamber such oxygenated blood encounters is the right atrium. It goes through the tricuspid valve to the right ventricle to the pulmonary arteries and then to the lungs where it is oxygenated. It returns to the heart through the pulmonary vein into the left atrium. It travels through the bicuspid valve to the left ventricle where it is pumped through the aorta to all parts of the body.

Sinoatrial node (SA node) - the pacemaker of the heart. Located on the right atrium, it is responsible for contraction of the right and left atrium.

Atrioventricular node (AV node) - located on the left ventricle, it is responsible for contraction of the ventricles.

Blood vessels include:

arteries - lead away from the heart. All arteries carry oxygenated blood except the pulmonary artery going to the lungs. Arteries are under high pressure.

arterioles - arteries branch off to form smaller arterioles.

capillaries - arterioles branch off to form tiny capillaries that reach every cell. Blood moves slowly through capillaires due to their small size; only one red blood cell may pass at a time to allow for diffusion of gases into and out of cells. Nutrients are also absorbed by the cells from the capillaries.

venules - capillaries combine to form larger venules. The vessels are now carrying waste products from the cells and deoxygenated blood.

veins - venules combine to form larger veins, leading back to the heart. Veins and venules have thinner walls than arteries because they are not under as much pressure. Veins contain unidirectional valves to prevent the backward flow of blood due to gravity.

Components of the blood include:

> **plasma** – 60% of the blood is plasma. It contains salts called electrolytes, nutrients, and waste. It is the liquid part of blood.
> **erythrocytes** - also called red blood cells; they contain hemoglobin, which carries oxygen molecules.
> **leukocytes** - also called white blood cells. White blood cells are larger than red blood cells. They are phagocytic and can engulf invaders. White blood cells are not confined to the blood vessels and can enter the interstitial fluid between cells.
> **platelets** - assist in blood clotting. Platelets are made in the bone marrow.

Blood clotting - the neurotransmitter that initiates blood vessel constriction following an injury is called serotonin. A material called prothrombin is converted to thrombin with the help of thromboplastin. The thrombin is then used to convert fibrinogen to fibrin, which traps red blood cells to form a scab and stop blood flow.

Lymphatic System (Immune System)

The immune system is responsible for defending the body against foreign invaders. There are two defense mechanisms: non specific and specific.

The **non-specific** immune mechanism has two lines of defenses. The first line of defense is the physical barriers in place on the body. These include the skin and mucous membranes. The skin prevents the penetration of bacteria and viruses as long as there are no abrasions on the skin. Mucous membranes form a protective barrier around the digestive, respiratory, and genitourinary tracts. In addition, the pH of the skin and mucous membranes inhibits the growth of many microbes. Mucous secretions (tears and saliva) wash away many microbes and contain lysozymes that kill many microbes.

The second line of defense includes white blood cells and the inflammatory response. White blood cells consume invaders by a process known as **phagocytosis**. Neutrophils make up about seventy percent of all white blood cells. Monocytes mature to become macrophages which are the largest phagocytic cells. Eosinophils are also phagocytic. Natural killer cells destroy the body's own infected cells instead of attacking the invading the microbe directly.

The other second line of defense mechanism is the inflammatory response. The blood supply to the injured area is increased, causing redness and heat. Swelling also typically occurs with inflammation. Histamine is released by basophils and mast cells when the cells are injured. This triggers the inflammatory response.

The **specific** immune mechanism recognizes specific foreign material and responds by destroying the specific invader. These mechanisms are individually specific, but in the aggregate are diverse in function. They are able to recognize individual pathogens. An **antigen** is any foreign particle that elicits an immune response. An **antibody** recognizes and latches onto antigens, clumping them together and hopefully destroying them. Memory of the invaders provides immunity upon further exposure.

Immunity is the body's ability to recognize and destroy an antigen before it causes harm. Active immunity develops after recovery from an infectious disease (e.g. chicken pox) or after a vaccination (e.g., mumps, measles, rubella). Passive immunity may be passed from one individual to another and is not permanent. A good example is the immunity passed from mother to nursing child. A baby's immune system is not well developed and the passive immunity they receive through nursing keeps them healthier.

The body makes two main responses after exposure to an antigen: humoral and cell-mediated.

1. **Humoral response** - Free antigens activate this response and B cells (lymphocytes from bone marrow) give rise to plasma cells that secrete antibodies and memory cells that will recognize future exposures to the same antigen. The antibodies defend against extracellular pathogens by binding to the antigen and making them an easy target for phagocytes to engulf and destroy. Antibodies are in a class of proteins called immunoglobulins. There are five major classes of immunoglobulins (Ig) involved in the humoral response: IgM, IgG, IgA, IgD, and IgE.

2. **Cell-mediated response** - Cells that have been infected activate T cells (lymphocytes from the thymus). These activated T cells defend against pathogens in the cells or against cancer cells by binding to the infected cells and destroying them along with the antigen. T cell receptors on the T helper cells recognize antigens bound to the body's own cells. T helper cells release IL-2 which stimulates other lymphocytes (cytotoxic T cells and B cells). Cytotoxic T cells kill infected host cells by recognizing specific antigens.

Vaccines are antigens given in very small amounts. They stimulate both humoral and cell-mediated responses and help memory cells recognize future exposure to the antigen so antibodies can be produced much faster.

The immune system attacks not only microbes, but also cells that are not native to the host. This response causes problems with skin grafts, organ transplantations, and blood transfusions. Antibodies to foreign blood and tissue types already exist in the body. If incompatible blood is transfused, these antibodies destroy the new blood cells. A similar reaction takes place when tissues or organs are transplanted.

The major histocompatibility complex (MHC) is responsible for the rejection of tissue and organ transplants. This complex is unique to each person. Cytotoxic T cells recognize the MHC on the transplanted tissue or organ as foreign and destroy the tissues. Various drugs are needed to suppress the immune system so this does not happen. Immunosuppression complicates medical care as the patient is more susceptible to opportunistic infection.

Excretory System

The function of the excretory system is to rid the body of nitrogenous wastes as a component of urea. The functional unit of excretion is the nephron, which make up the kidneys. Antidiuretic hormone (ADH) which is made in the hypothalamus and stored in the pituitary is released when differences in osmotic balance occur; ADH maintains the body's water balance. As the blood becomes more dilute, ADH release ends.

In the kidney, the Bowman's capsule contains the glomerulus, a tightly packed group of capillaries in the nephron. The glomerulus is under high pressure. Water, urea, salts, and other fluids leak out due to pressure into the Bowman's capsule. This fluid waste (filtrate) passes through the three regions of the nephron: the proximal convulated tubule, the loop of Henle, and the distal tubule. In the proximal convoluted tubule, unwanted molecules are secreted into the filtrate. In the loop of Henle, salt is actively pumped out of the tube and much water is lost due to the hyperosmosity of the inner part (medulla) of the kidney. As the fluid enters the distal tubule, more water is reabsorbed. Urine forms in the collecting duct that leads to the ureter, and on to the bladder, where urine is stored. Urine is passed from the bladder through the urethra. The amount of water reabsorbed back into the body is dependent upon how much water an individual has consumed. Urine can be very dilute or very concentrated.

Endocrine System

The function of the **endocrine system** is to manufacture proteins called hormones. **Hormones** are released into the bloodstream and are carried to a target tissue where they stimulate an action. There are two classes of hormones: steroid and peptide. Steroid hormones come from cholesterol and include the sex hormones. Peptide hormones are derived from amino acids. Hormones are specific and fit receptors on the target tissue cell surface. The receptor activates an enzyme that converts ATP to cyclic AMP. Cyclic AMP (cAMP) is a second messenger and relays the message from the cell membrane to the nucleus. The genes found in the nucleus turn on or off to cause a specific reaction in response to the hormone signal.

Peptide hormones are made in the pituitary, kidneys, and pancreas. They include the following:

> **Follicle stimulating hormone (FSH)** – functions in production of sperm or egg cells
> **Luteinizing hormone (LH)** - functions in ovulation
> **Luteotropic hormone (LTH)** - assists in production of progesterone
> **Growth hormone (GH)** - stimulates growth
> **Antidiuretic hormone (ADH)** - assists in retention of water
> **Oxytocin** - stimulates labor contractions at birth and let-down of milk
> **Melatonin** - regulates circadian rhythms

Epinephrine (adrenalin) - causes fight or flight reaction of the nervous system

Thyroxin - increases metabolic rate

Calcitonin - removes calcium from the blood

Insulin - decreases glucose level in the blood

Glucagon - increases glucose level in the blood

Although you probably won't be tested on individual hormones, be aware that hormones work on a feedback system. The increase or decrease in one hormone may cause the increase or decrease in another.

Reproductive System

Gametogenesis is the production of the sperm and egg cells.

Spermatogenesis begins at puberty in the male. One spermatogonia, the diploid precursor of sperm, produces four sperm cells. The sperm mature in the seminiferous tubules located in the testes. **Oogenesis**, the production of egg cells (ova), is usually complete by the birth of a female. Egg cells are not released until menstruation begins at puberty. Meiosis forms one ovum with nearly all the cytoplasm and three polar bodies that are reabsorbed by the body. The ovum are stored in the ovaries and released each month from puberty to menopause.

Path of the sperm - Sperm are stored in the seminiferous tubules in the testes where they mature. Mature sperm are found in the epididymis located on top of the testes. During ejaculation, the sperm travel up the **vas deferens** where they mix with semen made in the prostate and seminal vesicles and travel out the urethra.

Path of the egg - eggs are stored in the ovaries. Ovulation releases the egg into the fallopian tubes, which are ciliated to move the egg along. Fertilization normally occurs in the fallopian tube. If pregnancy does not occur, the egg passes through the uterus and is expelled through the vagina during menstruation. Levels of progesterone and estrogen stimulate menstruation and are controlled by the implantation of a fertilized egg so menstruation does not occur.

Pregnancy - if fertilization occurs, the zygote implants in the uterus after about two to three days. Implantation promotes secretion of human chorionic gonadotrophin (HCG). This is what is detected in pregnancy tests. The HCG keeps the level of progesterone elevated to maintain the uterine lining in order to feed the developing embryo until the umbilical cord forms. Oxytocin, which causes labor contractions and dilation of the cervix, initiates labor. Prolactin and oxytocin cause the production of milk.

Skill 12.2 Analyzing systems involved in the regulation of physiological processes (e.g., nervous system, endocrine system)

The **central nervous system** (CNS) consists of the brain and spinal cord. The CNS is responsible for the body's response to environmental stimuli. The spinal cord is located inside the spine. It sends out motor commands for movement in response to stimuli. The brain is where responses to more complex stimuli occurs. The meninges are the connective tissues that protect the CNS. The CNS contains fluid filled spaces called ventricles. These ventricles are filled with cerebrospinal fluid which is formed in the brain. This fluid cushions the brain and circulates nutrients, white blood cells, and hormones. The CNS's response to stimuli is a reflex. The reflex is an unconscious, automatic response.

The **peripheral nervous system (PNS)** consists of the nerves that connect the CNS to the rest of the body. The sensory division brings information to the CNS from sensory receptors and the motor division sends signals from the CNS to effector cells. The motor division consists of the somatic nervous system and the autonomic nervous system. The somatic nervous system is controlled consciously in response to external stimuli. The autonomic nervous system is unconsciously controlled by the hypothalamus of the brain to regulate the internal environment. This system is responsible for the movement of smooth and cardiac muscles as well as the muscles for other organ systems.

The function of the **endocrine system** is to manufacture proteins called hormones. **Hormones** are released into the bloodstream and are carried to a target tissue where they stimulate an action. There are two classes of hormones: steroid and peptide. Steroid hormones come from cholesterol and include the sex hormones. Peptide hormones are derived from amino acids. Hormones are specific and fit receptors on the target tissue cell surface. The receptor activates an enzyme that converts ATP to cyclic AMP. Cyclic AMP (cAMP) is a second messenger that relays the signal from the cell membrane to the nucleus. The genes found in the nucleus turn on or off to cause a specific response.

Hormones are secreted by endocrine cells which make up endocrine glands. The major endocrine glands and their hormones are as follows:

> **Hypothalamus** – located in the lower brain; signals the pituitary gland.
> **Pituitary gland** – located at the base of the hypothalamus; releases growth hormones and antidiuretic hormone (causing retention of water in the kidneys).
> **Thyroid gland** – located on the trachea; lowers blood calcium levels (calcitonin) and maintains metabolic processes (thyroxine).
> **Gonads** – located in the testes of the male and the ovaries of the female; testes release androgens to support sperm formation and ovaries release estrogens to stimulate uterine lining growth and progesterone to promote uterine lining growth.

> **Pancreas** – secretes insulin to lower blood glucose levels and glucagon to raise blood glucose levels.

The thyroid gland produces hormones that help maintain heart rate, blood pressure, muscle tone, digestion, and reproductive functions. The parathyroid glands maintain the calcium level in blood and the pancreas maintains glucose homeostasis by secreting insulin and glucagon. The three gonadal steroids, androgen (testosterone), estrogen, and progesterone, regulate the development of the male and female reproductive organs and secondary sex characteristics.

The **neuron** is the basic unit of the nervous system. It consists of an axon, which carries impulses away from the cell body to the tip of the neuron; the dendrite, which carries impulses toward the cell body; and the cell body, which contains the nucleus. Synapses are spaces between neurons. Chemicals called neurotransmitters are found close to the synapse. The myelin sheath, composed of Schwann cells, covers the neurons and provides insulation.

Nerve action depends on depolarization and an imbalance of electrical charges across the neuron. A polarized nerve has a positive charge outside the neuron. A depolarized nerve has a negative charge outside the neuron.

Neurotransmitters turn off the sodium pump, which results in depolarization of the membrane. This wave of depolarization (as it moves from neuron to neuron) carries an electrical impulse. This is actually a wave of opening and closing gates that allows for the flow of ions across the synapse. Nerves have an action potential. There is a threshold of the level of chemicals that must be met or exceeded in order for muscles to respond. This is called the "all or none" response.

Skill 12.3 Demonstrating knowledge of the tissues, organs, and systems that support and facilitate body movement (e.g., muscles, connective tissues, skeletal system)

See Skill 12.1

Skill 12.4 Analyzing the role of human body systems in supplying nutrition and oxygen to cells

See also Skill 12.1

The lungs are the respiratory surface of the human respiratory system. A dense net of capillaries contained just beneath the epithelium forms the respiratory surface. The surface area of the epithelium is about $100m^2$ in humans. Based on the surface area, the volume of air inhaled and exhaled is the tidal volume. This is normally about 500mL in adults. Vital capacity is the maximum volume the lungs can inhale and exhale. This is usually around 3400mL.

The respiratory system functions in the gas exchange of oxygen and carbon dioxide waste. It delivers oxygen to the bloodstream and picks up carbon dioxide for release out of the body. Air enters the mouth and nose, where it is warmed, moistened, and filtered of dust and particles. Cilia in the trachea trap unwanted material in mucus, which can be expelled. The trachea splits into two bronchial tubes and the bronchial tubes divide into smaller and smaller bronchioles in the lungs. The internal surface of the lung is composed of alveoli, which are thin walled air sacs. These allow for a large surface area for gas exchange. The alveoli are lined with capillaries. Oxygen diffuses into the bloodstream and carbon dioxide diffuses out of the capillaries to be exhaled out of the lungs.

The function of the digestive system is to break food down into nutrients and absorb the nutrients into the blood stream where they can be delivered to all cells of the body for use in cellular respiration.

Essential nutrients are those nutrients that the body needs but cannot make. There are four groups of essential nutrients: essential amino acids, essential fatty acids, vitamins, and minerals.

There are ten essential amino acids which humans need to obtain through diet. A lack of these amino acids results in protein deficiency. There are only a few essential fatty acids.

Vitamins are organic molecules essential for a nutritionally adequate diet. Nutritionists have identified thirteen vitamins essential to humans.

There are two groups of vitamins: water soluble (includes the vitamin B complex and vitamin C) and water insoluble (vitamins A, D and K). Vitamin deficiencies can cause severe health problems.

Unlike vitamins, minerals are inorganic molecules. Calcium is needed for bone construction and maintenance. Iron is important in cellular respiration and is a major component of hemoglobin.

Carbohydrates, fats, and proteins provide fuel for the regeneration of ATP. Water is necessary to keep the body hydrated.

Skill 12.5   Recognizing the characteristics of common diseases and disorders of the human body

Emphysema is a chronic obstructive pulmonary disease (COPD). These diseases make it difficult for a person to breathe. Airflow through the bronchial tubes is partially blocked, making breathing difficult. The primary cause of emphysema is cigarette smoke. People with a deficiency in alpha$_1$-antitrypsin protein production have a greater risk of developing emphysema and a greater risk of developing it at an earlier age. This protein helps protect the lungs from damage done by inflammation. This genetic deficiency is rare and can be tested for in individuals with a family history of the deficiency. There is no cure for emphysema, but there are treatments available. The best prevention against emphysema is to avoid smoking.

Nephritis usually occurs in children. Symptoms include hypertension, decreased renal function, hematuria, and edema. Glomerulonephritis (GN) generally is a more precise term to describe this disease. Nephritis is produced by an antigen-antibody complex that causes inflammation and cell proliferation. Normal kidney tissue is damaged and, if left untreated, nephritis can lead to kidney failure and death.

Cardiovascular diseases are the leading cause of death in the United States. Cardiac disease usually results in either a heart attack or a stroke. A heart attack is when cardiac muscle tissue dies, usually from coronary artery blockage. A stroke is when nervous tissue in the brain dies due to the blockage of arteries in the head.

Many heart attacks and strokes are caused by a disease called **atherosclerosis**. Plaques form on the inner walls of arteries, narrowing the area in which blood can flow. Arteriosclerosis is the hardening of the arteries from plaque accumulation. Atherosclerosis can be prevented by a healthy diet that limits lipids and cholesterol, and by regular exercise. High blood pressure (hypertension) promotes atherosclerosis. Diet, medication, and exercise can reduce high blood pressure and prevent atherosclerosis.

The immune system attacks not only microbes, but also cells that are not native to the host. This response causes difficulties with skin grafts, organ transplants, and blood transfusions. Antibodies to foreign blood and tissue types already exist in the body. If incompatible blood is transfused into the host, these antibodies destroy the new blood cells. A similar reaction occurs when tissues and organs are transplanted.

TEACHER CERTIFICATION STUDY GUIDE

The major histocompatibility complex (MHC) is responsible for the rejection of tissue and organ transplants. This complex is unique to each person. Cytotoxic T cells recognize the MHC on the transplanted tissue or organ as foreign and destroy these tissues. Various drugs are needed to suppress the immune system so this does not happen. Immunosuppression complicates medical care as the patient is more susceptible to opportunistic infection.

Autoimmune disease occurs when the body's own immune system destroys its own cells. Lupus, Grave's disease, and rheumatoid arthritis are examples of autoimmune diseases. There is no known way to prevent most autoimmune diseases. Immunodeficiency is a deficiency in either the humoral or cell mediated immune defenses. HIV is an example of an immunodeficiency disease.

Gastric ulcers are lesions in the stomach lining. Ulcers are mainly caused by bacteria, but are worsened by pepsin and acid if the ulcers are not healed quickly enough.

Appendicitis is the inflammation of the appendix. The appendix has no known function, is open to the intestine, and can be blocked by hardened stool or swollen tissue. The blocked appendix is susceptible to bacterial infections and inflammation leading to appendicitis. The swelling restricts blood supply, which in turns leads to organ tissue death. If left untreated, this leads to the rupture of the appendix, allowing the stool and infection to spill out into the abdomen. This condition is life threatening without immediate surgery. Symptoms of appendicitis include lower abdominal pain, nausea, loss of appetite, and fever.

Diabetes is the best known endocrine disorder. Diabetes is caused by a deficiency of insulin or a deficiency in insulin response, resulting in high blood glucose. Type I diabetes is an autoimmune disorder. The immune system attacks the cells of the pancreas, ending the ability to produce insulin. Treatment for type I diabetes consists of daily insulin injections. Type II diabetes usually occurs with age and/or obesity. There is usually a reduced response in target cells due to changes in insulin receptors or a deficiency of insulin. Type II diabetics need to monitor their blood glucose levels. Treatment usually includes dietary restrictions and exercise.

Hyperthyroidism is another disorder of the endocrine system, resulting in excessive secretion of thyroid hormones. Symptoms are weight loss, high blood pressure, and high body temperature. The opposite condition, hypothyroidism, causes weight gain, lethargy, and intolerance to cold.

BIOLOGY   90

There are many nervous system disorders. **Parkinson's disease** is caused by the degeneration of the basal ganglia in the brain. This causes a breakdown in the transmission of motor impulses to the muscles. Symptoms include tremors, slow movement, and muscle rigidity. Progression of Parkinson's disease occurs in five stages: early, mild, moderate, advanced, and severe. In the severe stage, the person is confined to a bed or chair. There is no cure for Parkinson's disease. Private stem cell research is underway to find a cure for Parkinson's disease.

COMPETENCY 13.0 UNDERSTAND POPULATIONS AND COMMUNITIES

Skill 13.1 Identifying the basic requirements of organisms for life (e.g., nutrition, space, habitat)

In order to survive, organisms must be able to meet several basic needs. They must be able to obtain energy and avoid being used as energy, obtain and conserve water, and find a space in which they can survive the extremes of abiotic factors.

Organisms obtain food in a variety of methods depending largely on the organism and the environment. Some single-celled organisms obtain food by crawling toward prey, engulfing it, and digesting it internally, while others make their own food by using energy from the sun in the same manner as plants. The food web demonstrates how animals obtain food, having to catch and digest prey or energy-rich organic substances in order to obtain the nutrients and energy to survive.

Finding a space to live in is a matter of survival of the fittest and the ability of organisms to co-exist in the same space. As environmental factors change organisms are often forced to look for new space. They are successful if they are not prey to the predators in the new space, can obtain the water and food they need to survive, and can withstand the environmental extremes of their new habitat.

Skill 13.2 Niche

The term 'niche' describes the relational position of a species or population in an ecosystem. Niche includes how a population responds to the abundance of its resources and enemies (e.g., by growing when resources are abundant and predators, parasites, and pathogens are scarce).

Niche also considers the life history of an organism, habitat, and place in the food chain. According to the competitive exclusion principle, no two species can occupy the same niche in the same environment for a long time.

The full range of environmental conditions (biological and physical) under which an organism can exist describes its fundamental niche. Because of the pressure from superior competitors, organisms often are driven to occupy a niche much narrower than their previous niche. This restricted range is known as the 'realized niche'.

Examples of niche:

1. Oak trees:
- live in forests
- absorb sunlight by photosynthesis
- provide shelter for many animals
- act as support for creeping plants
- serve as a source of food for animals
- cover their ground with dead leaves in the autumn

If the oak trees were cut down or destroyed by fire or storms they would no longer be doing their job and this would have a disastrous effect on all the other organisms living in the same habitat.

2. Hedgehogs:
- eat a variety of insects and other invertebrates which live underneath the dead leaves and twigs in the garden
- the spines are a superb environment for fleas and ticks
- put the nitrogen back into the soil when they urinate
- eat slugs and protect plants from them

If there were no hedgehogs around, the population of slugs would explode and the nutrients in the dead leaves and twigs would not be recycled.

Skill 13.3 Analyzing basic characteristics of populations (e.g., distribution, density) and interpreting population growth curves

Zero population growth occurs when the birth and death rates are equal in a population. Exponential growth rate occurs when there is an abundance of resources and the growth rate is at its maximum, called the intrinsic rate of increase. This relationship can be graphically presented as a growth curve.

An exponentially growing population starts off with little initial change and then rapidly increases without limit.

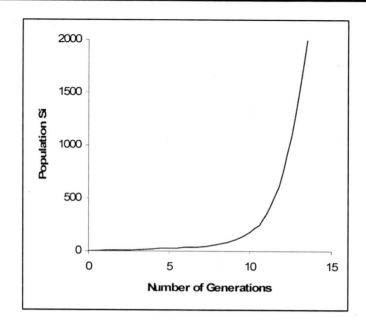

Logistic population growth incorporates the carrying capacity into the growth rate. As a population reaches the carrying capacity, the growth rate begins to slow down and level off. The carrying capacity is the theoretical maximum population that the environment can sustain over the long term.

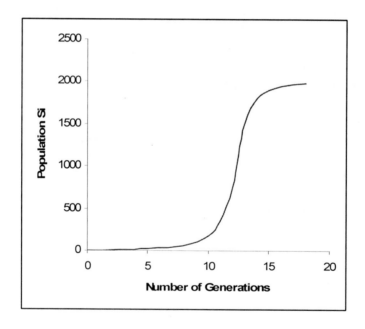

Many populations approximate the logistic model of population growth. Human population growth, however, more closely approximates an exponentially growing population. Eventually, the carrying capacity of the Earth will be reached, and the growth rate will level off. How and when this will occur remains a topic of debate.

Population density is the number of individuals per unit area or volume. The spacing pattern of individuals in an area is dispersion. **Dispersion patterns** can be clumped, with individuals grouped in patches; uniform, where individuals are approximately equidistant from each other; or random.

Population densities are usually estimated based on a few representative plots. Aggregation of a population in a relatively small geographic area can have detrimental effects to the environment. Food, water, and other resources will be rapidly consumed, resulting in a potentially unstable environment. Usually, a low population density is less harmful to the environment. The use of natural resources will be more dispersed, allowing the environment to recover and continue typical growth.

Skill 13.4 Demonstrating knowledge of factors that influence population size and growth rates (e.g., carrying capacity, limiting factors)

A **population** is a group of individuals of a single species that live in the same general area. Many factors can influence population size and population growth rate. Population size can depend on the total number of organisms a habitat can support. This is the **carrying capacity** of the environment. Once the habitat runs out of food, water, shelter, or space, the population stabilizes at or near the carrying capacity.

Limiting factors can impact population growth. As a population increases, the competition for resources is more intense, and the growth rate declines. This is a **density-dependent** growth factor. The carrying capacity usually depends on a combination of density-dependent factors. **Density-independent factors** affect individuals regardless of population size. The weather and climate are good examples. For example, a heat wave may kill many individuals from a population that has not reached its carrying capacity.

Skill 13.5 Analyzing the relationships among organisms in a community (e.g., predator/prey, symbiosis, parasitism)

Many interactions may occur between different species living together. Predation, parasitism, competition, commensalism, and mutualism are the different types of relationships populations have amongst each other.

Predation and **parasitism** result in a benefit for one species and a detriment for the other. Predation is when a predator kills or injures its prey. The common conception of predation is of a carnivore consuming other animals, though this is only one form of predation. Although not always resulting in the death of the plant, herbivores eating plants is another form of predation. Some animals eat enough of a plant to cause death. Parasitism involves a predator that lives on or in its host, causing detrimental effects to the host. Viral infection of a host is an example of parasitism. Many plants and animals have defenses against predators. For example, some plants have poisonous chemicals that, if ingested, will harm the predator and some animals are camouflaged so they are harder to detect.

Competition is when two or more species in a community utilize the same resources. Competition is usually detrimental to both populations. Competition is often difficult to find in nature because competition between two populations is rarely stable over a long period of time—either the less capable population vanishes or one population will adapt to utilize other available resources.

Symbiosis is when two species live close together. Parasitism, described above, is one example of symbiosis. **Commensalism** is a form of symbiosis where one species benefits without harmful effects to the other sepcies. **Mutualism** is a form of symbiosis where both species benefit. Species involved in mutualistic relationships must coevolve to maintain the mutualistic relationship. For example, the grouper fish and a particular species of shrimp live in a mutualistic relationship. The shrimp feed off parasites living on the grouper. Thus, the shrimp are fed and the grouper is freed of ecto-parasites. Many microorganisms have developed mutualistic relationships.

COMPETENCY 14.0 UNDERSTAND THE FLOW OF MATTER AND ENERGY THROUGH ECOSYSTEMS

Skill 14.1 Recognizing the characteristics of biogeochemical cycles in ecosystems and biomes (e.g., carbon, water, oxygen, nitrogen, phosphorus)

Biogeochemical cycles are nutrient cycles that involve both biotic and abiotic factors.

Water cycle - Two percent of all water is fixed in ice in or the bodies of organisms. Available liquid water includes surface water (e.g., lakes, oceans, rivers) and ground water (e.g., aquifers, wells). Ninety-six percent of all available water is ground water. The water cycle is driven by solar energy. Water is recycled through the processes of evaporation and precipitation. The water present on earth now is the water that has been here since our atmosphere formed.

Carbon cycle - Ten percent of all available carbon in the air (in the form of carbon dioxide gas) is fixed by photosynthesis. Plants fix carbon in the form of glucose. Animals eat the plants and are able to obtain carbon. When animals release carbon dioxide through respiration, the plants again have a source of carbon for further fixation.

Nitrogen cycle – Nitrogen gas composes 80% of the atmosphere. Nitrogen must be fixed and taken out of the gaseous form in order to be incorporated into an organism. Only a few genera of bacteria have the correct enzymes to break the triple covalent bond between nitrogen atoms in a process called nitrogen fixation. These bacteria live within the roots of legumes (e.g., peas, beans, alfalfa) and add nitrogen to the soil where it may be taken up by plants. Nitrogen is necessary to make amino acids and the nitrogenous bases of DNA.

Phosphorus cycle - Phosphorus exists as a mineral and is not found in the atmosphere. Fungi and plant roots have a structure called mycorrhizae that are able to fix insoluble phosphates into useable phosphorus. Urine and decayed matter return phosphorus to the earth where it again can be fixed by mycorrhizae. Phosphorus is needed for the backbone of DNA, for phospholipid construction, and for ATP manufacturing.

Oxygen is recycled throughout the biosphere. Plants release oxygen as a byproduct of photosynthesis. Animals utilize oxygen and release carbon dioxide as their byproduct. This carbon dioxide is then utilized by the plants during photosynthesis, and the cycle begins again.

Skill 14.2 Analyzing the roles of organisms in biogeochemical cycles and the flow of matter through different types of ecosystems

The basic stability of ecosystems depends on the interaction and contributions of a wide variety of species. For example, all living organisms require nitrogen to live. Only a select few species of microorganisms can convert atmospheric nitrogen into a form that is usable by most other organisms (nitrogen fixation). Thus, humans and all other organisms depend on the existence of nitrogen-fixing microbes. In addition, the cycling of carbon, oxygen, and water depends on the aggregate contribution of many different types of plants, animals, and microorganisms. Finally, the existence and functioning of a diverse range of species creates healthy, stable ecosystems. Stable ecosystems are more adaptable and less susceptible to extreme events like floods and droughts.

Skill 14.3 Analyzing the types, sources, and flow of energy through different trophic levels (e.g., producers, consumers, and decomposers) and between organisms and the physical environment in aquatic and terrestrial ecosystems

Trophic levels describe the feeding relationships between species and the subsequent energy flow and chemical cycling.

Autotrophs are the primary producers of the ecosystem. **Producers** mainly consist of plants and algae. **Primary consumers** are the next trophic level. The primary consumers are the herbivores that eat plants or algae. **Secondary consumers** are the carnivores that eat the primary consumers. **Tertiary consumers** eat the secondary consumers. Trophic levels may go on, depending on the ecosystem. **Decomposers** are consumers that feed off animal waste and dead organisms. This pathway of food transfer is the food chain, and the complex interconnected relationships between the various trophic levels are collectively referred to as the food web.

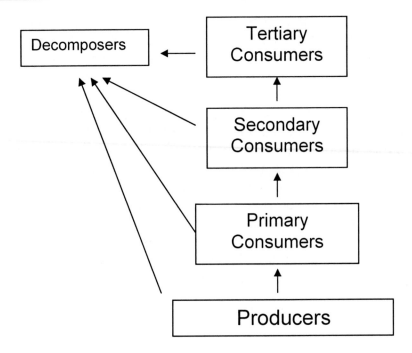

Most food chains are more elaborate, becoming food webs.

Energy is lost as the trophic levels progress from producer to tertiary consumer. The amount of energy that is transferred between trophic levels is called the ecological efficiency. The visual of this energy flow is represented in a **pyramid of productivity**.

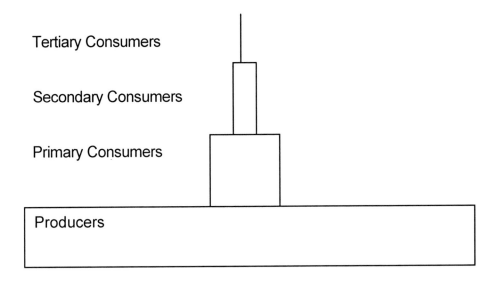

The **biomass pyramid** represents the total dry weight of organisms at each trophic level. A **pyramid of numbers** is a representation of the population size at each trophic level. The producers, being the most populous, are on the bottom of this pyramid with the tertiary consumers on the top with the fewest numbers.

An ecosystem is the collection of all components and processes that define a portion of the biosphere. Ecosystems include both biotic (living) and abiotic (non-living) components. While the behavior of individual organisms in an ecosystem impacts other members of the ecosystem, ecosystems themselves are also interrelated. Because the boundaries of ecosystems are not fixed, organisms and other ecosystem products and components can move freely between ecosystems. For example, the waste products from a terrestrial ecosystem may enter an aquatic ecosystem, changing environmental characteristics. In addition, any ecosystem process that alters the global environment impacts all other ecosystems. For example, the production of greenhouse gases that deplete the ozone layer and promote global warming impacts the global climate, altering the characteristics of ecosystems across the globe.

COMPETENCY 15.0   **UNDERSTAND TYPES AND CHARACTERISTICS OF ECOSYSTEMS AND BIOMES AND FACTORS INFLUENCING THEIR CHANGE OVER TIME**

Skill 15.1 Recognizing common patterns of interdependence and interrelationships among species in an ecosystem (e.g., the role of producers, consumers, and decomposers)

Autotrophs are the primary producers of the ecosystem. **Producers** mainly consist of plants and algae. **Primary consumers** are the next trophic level. The primary consumers are the herbivores that eat plants or algae. **Secondary consumers** are the carnivores that eat the primary consumers. **Tertiary consumers** eat the secondary consumers. Trophic levels may go on, depending on the ecosystem. **Decomposers** are consumers that feed off animal waste and dead organisms. This pathway of food transfer is the food chain.

Decomposers recycle the carbon accumulated in durable organic material that does not immediately proceed to the carbon cycle. Ammonification is the decomposition of organic nitrogen back to ammonia. This process in the nitrogen cycle is carried out by aerobic and anaerobic bacterial and fungal decomposers. Decomposers add phosphorous back to the soil by decomposing the excretion of animals.

Skill 15.2 Identifying the biotic and abiotic factors that impact an ecosystem

Abiotic and biotic factors play a role in succession. **Biotic factors** are living things in an ecosystem (e.g., plants, animals, fungi, protists, and bacteria). **Abiotic factors** are non-living aspects of an ecosystem (e.g., soil quality, rainfall, and temperature).

Abiotic factors influence succession by way of the species that colonize the area. Certain species will or will not survive depending on the weather, climate, or soil makeup. Biotic factors such as inhibition of one species due to another may occur. This may be due to some form of competition between the species.

Skill 15.3 Recognizing types and characteristics of aquatic and terrestrial biomes and the types of flora and fauna in those biomes

An ecosystem includes all living things in a specific area and the non-living things that influence them. The term **biome** is usually used to classify the general types of ecosystems in the world. Each biome contains distinctive organisms best adapted to that natural environment (including geological make-up, latitude, and altitude). All the living things in a biome are naturally in equilibrium and disturbances in any one element may cause repercussion throughout the system It should be noted that these biomes may have various names in different areas. For example steppe, savanna, veld, prairie, outback, and scrub are all regional terms that describe the same biome—grassland.

The major terrestrial biomes are desert, grassland, tundra, boreal forest, tropical rainforest, and temperate forest.

Desert

Deserts exist at any location that receives less that 50 cm of precipitation a year. Despite their lack of water and often desolate appearance, the soils, though loose and silty, tend to be rich and specialized plants and animals do populate deserts. Plant species include xerophytes and succulents. Animals tend to be non-mammalian and small (e.g., reptiles and insects). Large animals are not able to find sufficient shade in the desert and mammals, in general, are not well adapted to storing water and withstanding heat. Deserts may be either hot or cold. Hot and dry deserts are what we typically envision when we think of a desert and they occur throughout the world. Hot deserts are located in northern Africa, southwestern United States, and the Middle East. Cold deserts have similarly little vegetation and small animals and are located near the poles in Antarctica, Greenland, much of central Asia, and the Arctic. Both types of deserts do receive precipitation in the winter, though it is in the form of rain in hot deserts and the form of snow in cold deserts.

Grassland

As the name suggests, grassland includes large expanses of grass with only a few shrubs or trees. There are both tropical and temperate grasslands.

Tropical grasslands cover much of Australia, South America, and India. The weather is warm year-round with moderate rainfall. However, the rainfall is concentrated in half the year and drought and fires are common in the other half of the year. These fires serve to renew rather than destroy areas within tropical grasslands. This type of grassland supports a large variety of animals from insects to mammals both large and small such as squirrels, mice, gophers, giraffes, zebras, kangaroos, lions, and elephants.

Temperate grasslands receive even less rain than tropical grasslands and are found in South Africa, Eastern Europe, and the western United States. As with tropical grasslands, periods of drought and fire serve to renew the ecosystem. Differences in temperature also differentiate the temperate from the tropical grasslands. Temperate grasslands are cooler in general and experience even colder temperatures in winter. These grasslands support similar types of animals as the tropical grasslands: prairie dogs, deer, mice, coyotes, hawks, snakes, and foxes.

The savanna is grassland with scattered individual trees. Dominant plants of the savanna include shrubs and grasses. Temperatures range from 0 - 25 °C in the savanna depending on its location. Rainfall is from 90 to 150 cm per year. The savanna is a transitional biome between the rain forest and the desert that is located in central South America, southern Africa, and parts of Australia.

Tundra

Tundra is treeless plain with extremely low temperatures (-28 to 15 °C) and little vegetation or precipitation. Rainfall is limited, ranging from 10 to 15 cm per year. A layer of permanently frozen subsoil, called permafrost, is found in the tundra. The permafrost means that no vegetation with deep root systems can exist in the tundra, but low shrubs, mosses, grasses, and lichen are able to survive. These plants grow low and close together to resist the cold temperature and strong winds. The few animals that live in the tundra are adapted to the cold winters (via layers of subcutaneous fat, hibernation, or migration) and raise their young quickly during the summers. Such species include lemmings, caribou, arctic squirrels and foxes, polar bears, cod, salmon, mosquitoes, falcons, and snow birds.

Both arctic and alpine tundra exist, though their characteristics are extremely similar and are distinguished mainly by the location (arctic tundra is located near the North Pole, while alpine tundra is found in the world's highest mountains).

Polar tundra or permafrost has temperature ranges from -40 to 0 °C. It rarely gets above freezing. Rainfall is below 10 cm per year. Most water is bound up as ice. Life is limited.

Forests

There are three types of forest, all characterized by the abundant growth of trees, but with difference in climate, flora, and fauna.

Boreal forest (taiga)

These forests are located throughout northern Europe, Asia, and North America, near the pole. The climate typically consists of short, rainy summers followed by long, cold winters with snow. The trees in boreal forests are adapted to the cold winters and are typically evergreens including pine, fir, and spruce. The trees are so thick that there is little undergrowth. A number of animals are adapted to life in the boreal forest, including many mammals such as bear, moose, wolves, chipmunks, weasels, mink, and deer. These coniferous forests have temperatures ranging from -24 to 22 °C. Rainfall is between 35 to 40 cm per year. This is the largest terrestrial biome.

Tropical rainforest

Tropical rainforests are located near the equator and are typically warm and wet throughout the entire year. The temperature is constant (25 °C) and the length of daylight is about 12 hours. The precipitation is frequent and occurs roughly evenly during the year. In a tropical rainforest, rainfall exceeds 200 cm per year. Tropical rainforests have abundant, diverse species of plants and animals. A tropical dry forest gets scarce rainfall and a tropical deciduous forest has wet and dry seasons. The soil is surprisingly nutrient-poor and most of the biomass is located within the trees themselves. The vegetation is highly diverse including many trees with shallow roots, orchids, vines, ferns, mosses, and palms. Animals are similarly plentiful and varied and include all type of birds, reptiles, bats, insects, and small to medium sized mammals.

Temperate forest

These forests have well defined winters and summers with precipitation throughout the year. Temperate forests are common in Western Europe, eastern North America, and parts of Asia. Common trees include deciduous species such as oak, beech, maple, and hickory. Unlike the boreal forests, the canopy in the temperate forest is not particularly heavy and so various smaller plants occupy the understory. Mammals and birds are the predominate form of animal life. Typical species include squirrels, rabbits, skunks, deer, bobcats, and bear. Temperatures range from -24 to 38 °C. Rainfall is between 65 and 150 cm per year.

A subtype of temperate forests are *chaparral forests*. Chaparral forests experience mild, rainy winters and hot, dry summers. Trees do not grow well here. Spiny shrubs dominate. Regions include the Mediterranean, the California coastline, and southwestern Australia.

Aquatic ecosystems

Aquatic ecosystems are, as the name suggests, ecosystems located within bodies of water. Aquatic biomes are divided between fresh water and marine. Freshwater ecosystems are closely linked to terrestrial biomes. Lakes, ponds, rivers, streams, and swamplands are examples of freshwater biomes. Marine areas cover 75% of the earth. This biome is organized by the depth of the water. The intertidal zone is from the tide line to the edge of the water. The littoral zone is from the water's edge to the open sea. It includes coral reef habitats and is the most densely populated area of the marine biome. The open sea zone is divided into the epipelagic zone and the pelagic zone. The epipelagic zone receives more sunlight and has a larger number of species.

The ocean floor is called the benthic zone and is populated with bottom feeders. Marine biomes include coral reefs, estuaries, and several systems within the oceans.

Oceans

Within the world's oceans, there are several separate zones, each with its own temperature profiles and unique species. These zones include intertidal, pelagic, benthic, and abyssal. The intertidal and pelagic zones are further distinguished by the latitude at which they occur (species have evolved to live in various temperature water which is closely correlated with latitude). The intertidal zone is the shore area, which is alternately under and above the water, depending on the tidal stage. Algae, mollusks, snails, crabs, and seaweed are all found in the intertidal zones. The pelagic zone is further from land but near the surface of the ocean. This zone is sometimes called the euphotic zone. Temperatures are much cooler than in the intertidal zone and organisms in this zone include surface seaweeds, plankton, various fish, whales, and dolphins. Further below the ocean's surface is the benthic zone, which is even colder and darker. Much seaweed is found in this zone, as well as bacteria, fungi, sponges, anemones, sea stars, and some fishes. Deeper still is the abyssal zone, which is the coldest and darkest area of the ocean and has high pressure and low oxygen content. Thermal vents found in the abyssal zone support chemosynthetic bacteria, which are in turn eaten by invertebrates and fishes.

Coral reefs

Coral reefs are located in warm, shallow water near large land masses. The best known example is the Great Barrier Reef off the coast of Australia. The coral itself is the predominant life form in the reefs and obtains its nutrients largely through photosynthesis (performed by the algae). Many other animal life forms also populate coral reefs: many species of fish, octopuses, sea stars, and urchins.

Estuaries

Estuaries are found where fresh and seawater meet, for instance where rivers flow into the oceans. Many species have evolved to thrive in the brackish waters that exist in estuaries. The species include marsh grasses, mangrove trees, oysters, crabs, and certain waterfowl.

Ponds and Lakes

Many varied ecosystems occur in ponds and lakes. This is not surprising since lakes vary in size and location. Some lakes are even seasonal, lasting just a few months each year. Additionally, within lakes there are zones, comparable to those in oceans. The littoral zone, located near the shore and at the top of the lake, is the warmest and lightest zone. Organisms in this zone typically include aquatic plants and insects, snails, clams, fish, and amphibians. Further from land, but still at the surface of the lake is the limnetic zone.

Plankton is abundant in the limnetic zone and it is at the bottom of the food chain in this zone, ultimately supporting freshwater fish of all sizes. Deeper in the lake is the profundal zone, which is cooler and darker. Plankton also serves as a valuable food source in this zone since much of it dies and falls to the bottom of the lake. Again, small fish eat this plankton.

Rivers and Streams

This biome includes moving bodies of water. As expected, the organisms found within streams vary according to latitude and geological features. Additionally, characteristics of the stream change as it flows from its headwaters to the sea. Also, as the depth of rivers increases, zones similar to those seen in the ocean are seen. That is, different species live in the upper, sunlit areas (e.g., algae, top feeding fish, and aquatic insects) then in the darker, bottom areas (e.g., catfish, carp, and microbes).

Wetlands

Wetlands are the only aquatic biome that is partially land-based. Wetlands are areas of standing water in which aquatic plants grow. These species, called hydrophytes, are adapted to extremely humid and moist conditions and include lilies, cattails, sedges, cypress, and black spruce. Animal life in wetlands includes insects, amphibians, reptiles, many birds, and a few small mammals. Though wetlands are usually classified as a freshwater biome, there are in fact salt marshes that support shrimp, various fish, and grasses.

Skill 15.4 Analyzing human effects on ecosystems

Humans are continuously searching for new places to form communities. This encroachment on the environment leads to the destruction of wildlife communities.

Conservationists focus on endangered species, but the primary focus should be on protecting entire biomes. If a biome is ruined, the displaced wildlife dies or invades another biome.

Nature preserves established by governments aim at protecting small parts of biomes. While beneficial in the conservation of a few areas, the majority of the environment is still unprotected.

The human population has been growing exponentially for centuries. People are living longer and healthier lives than ever before. Better health care and nutrition practices have helped increase long-term survival of many populations.

Human activity greatly impacts nutrient cycles by removing nutrients from one part of the biosphere and adding them to another. This results in nutrient depletion in one area and nutrient excess in another, and it can impact water systems, crops, wildlife, and humans.

Humans are responsible for the depletion of the ozone layer. This depletion is thought to be largely due to chemicals used for refrigeration and aerosols. The consequences of ozone depletion likely will be severe. Ozone protects the Earth from the majority of ultraviolet solar radiation. An increase of ultraviolet solar radiation will promote skin cancer and likely cause many unpredictable effects on wildlife and plants.

Humans have a tremendous impact on the world's natural resources. The world's natural water supplies are seriously impacted by human use. Waterways are major sources for recreation and freight transportation. Oil and wastes from boats and cargo ships pollute the aquatic environment. The aquatic plant and animal life is negatively impacted by this contamination.

Deforestation for urban development has resulted in the extinction or relocation of several species of plants and animals. Animals are forced to leave their forest homes or perish amongst the ecological destruction. The number of plant and animal species that have become extinct due to deforestation is unknown. Scientists have only identified a fraction of the species on Earth. It is known that if the destruction of natural resources continues unabated, there may be no or very few plants or animals successfully reproducing in the wild.

Skill 15.5 Recognizing processes and patterns of ecological succession

Succession is an orderly process of replacing a community that has been damaged or has begun where no life previously existed. Primary succession occurs where life never existed before, for example on a new volcanic island. Secondary succession takes place in communities that were once flourishing but were seriously disturbed but not totally destroyed. A climax community is a community that is established and flourishing.

Abiotic and biotic factors play a role in succession. **Biotic factors** are living things in an ecosystem (e.g., plants, animals, fungi, protists, and bacteria). **Abiotic factors** are non-living aspects of an ecosystem (e.g., soil quality, rainfall, and temperature).

Abiotic factors impact succession by way of the species that colonize the area. Certain species will or will not survive depending on the weather, climate, or soil makeup. Biotic factors such as inhibition of one species due to another may occur. This may be due to some form of competition between the species.

Skill 15.6 Recognizing the concept of limiting factors (e.g., light intensity, temperature, mineral availability) and the effects that they have on the productivity and complexity of different ecosystems

A **limiting factor** is a component of a biological process that determines how quickly or slowly the process proceeds. Photosynthesis is the main biological process determining the rate of ecosystem productivity—the rate at which an ecosystem creates biomass. Thus, in evaluating the productivity of an ecosystem, potential limiting factors are light intensity, water, gas concentrations, and mineral availability. The Law of the Minimum states that the required factor in a given process that is most scarce controls the rate of the process.

One potential limiting factor of ecosystem productivity is light intensity because photosynthesis requires light energy. Light intensity can limit productivity in two ways. Too little light limits the rate of photosynthesis because the required energy is not available. Conversely, too much light can damage the photosynthetic system of plants and microorganisms thus slowing the rate of photosynthesis. Decreased photosynthesis equals decreased productivity.

Another potential limiting factor of ecosystem productivity is gas concentrations. Photosynthesis requires carbon dioxide. Thus, increased concentration of carbon dioxide often results in increased productivity. While carbon dioxide is often not the ultimate limiting factor of productivity, increased concentration can indirectly increase rates of photosynthesis in several ways. First, increased carbon dioxide concentration often increases the rate of nitrogen fixation (available nitrogen is another limiting factor of productivity). Second, increased carbon dioxide concentration can decrease the pH of rain, improving the water source of photosynthetic organisms.

Finally, mineral availability also limits ecosystem productivity. Plants require adequate amounts of nitrogen and phosphorus to build many cellular structures. The availability of the inorganic minerals phosphorus and nitrogen often is the main limiting factor of plant biomass production. In other words, in a natural environment phosphorus and nitrogen availability most often limits ecosystem productivity, rather than carbon dioxide concentration or light intensity.

COMPETENCY 16.0 UNDERSTAND THE CHARACTERISTICS OF SCIENTIFIC KNOWLEDGE AND THE PROCESS OF SCIENTIFIC INQUIRY

Skill 16.1 Demonstrating knowledge of the nature, purpose, and characteristics of science (e.g., reliance on verifiable evidence) and the limitations of science in terms of the kinds of questions that can be answered

Science is a body of knowledge systematically derived from study, observation, and experimentation. Its goal is to identify and establish principles and theories that may be applied to solve problems. Pseudoscience, on the other hand, is belief that is not supported by hard evidence but that nevertheless is presented as science. In other words, scientific methodology has not been applied to pseudoscientific statements. Some classic examples of pseudoscience include witchcraft, alien encounters, or any topic putatively explained by hearsay.

Science can only answer certain types of questions because the scientific method requires observable phenomena. That is, only testable hypotheses are valid for scientific investigation. Variables in a system must be controllable to an extent that allows experimentation to determine their effects. If variables cannot be artificially controlled, several different naturally occurring systems in which the desired variable differs can be studied. This is often the case in environmental biology.

Scientific research serves two primary purposes–
1. To investigate and acquire knowledge that is theoretical *and*
2. To do research which is of practical value.

Science is in a unique position to be able to serve humanity. Scientific research comes from inquiry. An inquiring mind is trying to find answers. A person who is inquisitive asks questions and wants to find answers. The two most important questions–why and how–are the starting points of all inquiry.

Scientific research uses either direct observation or the scientific method to answer questions. Researchers follow the scientific method, which consists of a series of steps designed to solve a problem.

The aim of the scientific method is to eliminate any bias or prejudice that the scientist or researcher may bring to the process. The scientific method is designed to achieve the maximum elimination of bias.

Scientific research is clearly different from learning in other subject areas. Science demands evidence and requires experimentation to prove one's hypotheses. Science does not, however, answer all our questions. It is up to us to use the information science provides and make our own decisions according to our beliefs and societal mores.

Skill 16.2 Recognizing the difference between a scientific hypothesis and a scientific theory

Results obtained through scientific experimentation must be repeatable. Experimentation leads to theories that can be disproved and changed. Science depends on communication, agreement, and disagreement among scientists. It is composed of hypotheses, theories, and laws.

- **Hypothesis** - An unproved theory or educated guess followed by research to best explain a phenomena. Once supported by scientific evidence, a hypothesis becomes a theory.

- **Theory** - A statement of principles or relationships relating to a natural event or phenomenon, which have been scientifically verified and generally accepted.

- **Law** - An explanation of events that occur with uniformity under the same conditions (e.g., laws of nature, law of gravitation). Laws differ from theories in that laws are analytic statements, generally supported by empirically determined constants.

Skill 16.3 Recognizing the dynamic nature of scientific knowledge through the continual testing and revision of hypotheses

The first step in scientific inquiry is posing a question based upon observation. Next, a hypothesis is formed to provide a plausible explanation. An experiment is then proposed and performed to test the hypothesis. A comparison between the predicted and observed results either supports or discredits the original hypothesis. Conclusions are then formed and the hypothesis is modified as necessary.

Science is limited by the available technology. An example of this would be the relationship between the discovery of the cell and the invention of the microscope. As our technology improves, more hypotheses will become theories and possibly laws. Data collection methods also limit scientific inquiry. Data may be interpreted differently on different occasions. Limitations of scientific methodology produce explanations that change as new technologies emerge.

Skill 16.4 Determining an appropriate scientific hypothesis or investigative design for addressing a given problem

The scientific method is particularly useful for determining 'cause and effect' relationships. Thus, appropriate hypotheses are often of this nature. The hypothesis is simply a prediction about a certain behavior that occurs in a system. Researchers then change variables to determine whether the hypothesis generally is correct. For instance, let's consider several identical potted African violets and suppose we have lights of different color, fertilizer, water, and a variety of common household items. Below are some possible questions, phrased as hypotheses, and a bit about why they are or are not valid.

1. African violets will grow taller in blue light than they will in red light.

This hypothesis is valid because we could easily test it by growing some violets in blue light and some in red light. We could easily observe the results by measuring the height of the violets.

2. Invisible microbes cause the leaves of African violets to turn yellow.

This hypothesis is not valid because we cannot know whether a given violet is infected with the microbe. We could test this hypothesis if we had appropriate technology to detect the presence of the microbe.

3. Lack of water will stop the growth of African violets.

This hypothesis is also valid because we could test it by denying water to some violets while continuing to water others. We may need to refine the hypothesis to define more specifically how we will measure growth, but presumably, we could do this easily.

4. African violets will not grow well in swamps.

This hypothesis is not valid in our specific situation because we have only potted plants. We could test this hypothesis by actually attempting to grow African violets in a swamp, but that lies outside the proposed scenario.

Skill 16.5 Demonstrating knowledge of the principles and procedures for designing and carrying out scientific investigations (e.g., changing one variable at a time)

The procedure used to obtain data is important to the outcome. Experiments consist of **controls** and **variables**. A control is the experiment run under normal, non-manipulated conditions.

A variable is a factor or condition the scientist manipulates. In biology, the variable may be light, temperature, pH, time, etc. Scientists can use the differences in tested variables to make predictions or form hypotheses. Generally, only one variable should be tested at a time. In other words, one would not alter both the temperature and pH of the experimental subject.

An **independent variable** is one is the researcher directly changes or manipulates. This could be the amount of light given to a plant or the temperature at which bacteria is grown. The **dependent variable** is the factor that changes due to the influence of the independent variable.

Skill 16.6 Recognizing the importance of and strategies for avoiding bias in scientific investigations

Bias in scientific research can occur in the choice of what data to consider, in the reporting or recording of the data, and/or in the interpretation of the data. A scientist's nationality, sex, ethnic origin, age, or political convictions may influence his or her decision making and emphasis. For example, when studying a group of animals, male scientists may focus on the social behavior of the males and typically male characteristics whereas female scientists may focus on the social behavior or characteristics of the females.

Although we may not be able to avoid completely bias related to the investigator, the sample, the method, or the instrument in every case, it is important to know the possible sources of bias and how bias can influence the evidence. Moreover, scientists need to be attentive to possible bias in their own work as well as that of other scientists.

While we may not always be entirely objective, one precaution that we can take to guard against undetected bias is to have many different investigators or groups of investigators working on a project. The different research groups should consist of researchers of various nationalities, ethnic origins, ages, and political convictions and each group should include both males and females. It is also important to note one's aspirations, and to make a truthful approach to the data, even when grants, promotions, and notoriety are at risk.

Skill 16.7 Demonstrating knowledge of the unifying concepts (e.g., system, model, change, scale) of science

Math, science, and technology share many common themes. All three disciplines use models, diagrams, and graphs to simplify complex concepts for analysis and interpretation. Patterns observed in these systems lead to predictions based on these observations. The following are the concepts and processes generally recognized as common to all scientific disciplines:

- Systems, order, and organization
- Evidence, models, and explanation
- Constancy, change, and measurement
- Evolution and equilibrium
- Form and function

Systems, order, and organization

Because the natural world is so complex, the study of science involves the organization of items into smaller groups based on interaction or interdependence. We call these groups systems. Examples of organization are the periodic table of elements and the five-kingdom classification scheme for living organisms. Examples of systems are the solar system, cardiovascular system, Newton's laws of force and motion, and the laws of conservation.

Order refers to the behavior and measurability of organisms and events in nature. The arrangement of planets in the solar system and the life cycle of bacterial cells are examples of order.

Evidence, models, and explanations

Scientists use evidence and models to form explanations of natural events. Models are miniaturized representations of a larger event or system. Evidence is anything that furnishes proof.

Constancy, change, and measurement

Constancy and change describe the observable properties of natural organisms and events. Scientists use different systems of measurement to observe change and constancy. For example, the freezing and melting points of given substances and the speed of sound are constant under constant conditions. Growth, decay, and erosion are all examples of natural change.

Evolution and equilibrium

Evolution is the process of change over a long period of time. While biological evolution is the most common example, one can also classify technological advancement, changes in the universe, and changes in the environment as evolution.

Equilibrium is the state of balance between opposing forces of change. Homeostasis and ecological balance are examples of equilibrium.

Form and function

Form and function are properties of organisms and systems that are closely related. The function of an object usually dictates its form and the form of an object usually facilitates its function. For example, the form of the heart (e.g. muscle, valves) allows it to perform its function of circulating blood through the body.

COMPETENCY 17.0 UNDERSTAND SCIENTIFIC TOOLS, INSTRUMENTS, MATERIALS, AND SAFETY PRACTICES

Skill 17.1 Recognizing procedures for the safe and proper use of scientific tools, instruments, chemicals, and other materials in investigations

Light microscopes are commonly used in high school laboratory experiments. Total magnification is determined by multiplying the magnification of the ocular and the objective lenses. Oculars usually magnify 10X and objective lenses usually magnify 10X on low and 40X on high.

Procedures for the care and use of microscopes include:
- cleaning all lenses with lens paper only
- carrying microscopes with two hands (one on the arm and one on the base)
- always beginning on low power when focusing
- storing microscopes with the low power objective down
- always using a coverslip when viewing wet mount slides
- bringing the objective down to its lowest position and then focusing, moving up to avoid breaking the slide or scratching the lens

Wet mount slides should be made by placing a drop of water on the specimen and then putting a glass coverslip on top of the drop of water. Dropping the coverslip at a forty-five degree angle will help avoid air bubbles.

Chromatography uses the principles of capillarity to separate substances such as plant pigments. Molecules of a larger size will move slower up the paper, whereas smaller molecules will move more quickly producing lines of pigment.

An **indicator** is any substance used to assist in the classification of another substance. An example of an indicator is litmus paper. Litmus paper is a way to measure whether a substance is acidic or basic. Blue litmus turns pink when an acid is placed on it and pink litmus turns blue when a base is placed on it. pH paper is a more accurate measure of pH, with the paper turning different colors depending on the pH value.

Spectrophotometry measures percent of light at different wavelengths absorbed and transmitted by a pigment solution.

Centrifugation involves spinning substances at a high speed. The more dense part of a solution will settle to the bottom of the test tube, while the lighter material will stay on top. Centrifugation is used to separate whole blood into blood cells and plasma, with the heavier blood cells settling to the bottom.

Electrophoresis uses the electrical charges of molecules to separate them according to their size. The molecules, such as DNA or proteins, are pulled through a gel towards either the positive end of the gel box (if the material has a negative charge) or the negative end of the gel box (if the material has a positive charge). DNA is negatively charged and moves towards the positive charge.

All laboratory solutions should be prepared as directed in the lab manual. Care should be taken to avoid contamination. All glassware should be rinsed thoroughly with distilled water before use, and cleaned well after use. All solutions should be made with distilled water as tap water contains dissolved particles that may alter the results of an experiment. Unused solutions should be disposed of according to local disposal procedures.

The "Right to Know Law" covers science teachers who work with potentially hazardous chemicals. Briefly, the law states that employees must be informed of potentially toxic chemicals. An inventory must be made available if requested. The inventory must contain information about the hazards and properties of the chemicals. This inventory is to be checked against the "Substance List". Training must be provided on safe handling and interpretation of the Material Safety Data Sheet format.

The following chemicals are potential carcinogens and are not allowed in school facilities: Acrylonitriel, Arsenic compounds, Asbestos, Benzidine, Benzene, Cadmium compounds, Chloroform, Chromium compounds, Ethylene oxide, Ortho-toluidine, Nickle powder, and Mercury.

Chemicals should not be stored on bench tops or near heat sources. They should be stored in groups based on their reactivity with one another and in protective storage cabinets. All containers within the lab must be labeled. Suspected and known carcinogens must be labeled as such and stored in trays to contain leaks and spills.

Chemical waste should be disposed of in properly labeled containers. Waste should be separated based on its reactivity with other chemicals.

Biological material should never be stored near food or water used for human consumption. All biological material should be appropriately labeled. All blood and body fluids should be put in a well-constructed container with a secure lid to prevent leaking. All biological waste should be disposed of in biological hazardous waste bags.

Material Safety Data Sheets are available for every chemical and biological substance. These are available directly from the distribution company and the internet. Before using lab equipment, all lab workers should read and understand the equipment manuals.

Skill 17.2 Identifying appropriate units for measuring objects or substances

Most modern science uses the **metric system**, as it is universally accepted and allows easier comparison among experiments done by scientists around the world.

The meter is the basic metric unit of length; one meter is about 1.09 yards. The liter is the basic metric unit of volume; one liter is about 0.26 gallons. The gram is the basic metric unit of mass; one gram is about 0.0022 pounds.

The following prefixes define multiples of the basic metric units.

deca	10x the base unit	deci	1/10 the base unit
hecto	100x the base unit	centi	1/100 the base unit
kilo	1,000x the base unit	milli	1/1,000 the base unit
mega	1,000,000x the base unit	micro	1/1,000,000 the base unit
giga	1,000,000,000x the base unit	nano	1/1,000,000,000 the base unit
tera	1,000,000,000,000x the base unit	pico	1/1,000,000,000,000 the base unit

The common instrument used for measuring volume is the graduated cylinder. The standard unit of measurement is milliliters (mL). To ensure accurate measurement, it is important to read the liquid in the cylinder at the bottom of the meniscus, the curved surface of the liquid.

The common instrument used in measuring mass is the triple beam balance. The triple beam balance can accurately measure tenths of a gram and can estimate hundredths of a gram.

The ruler and meter stick are the most commonly used instruments for measuring length. As with all scientific measurements, standard units of length are metric.

Skill 17.3 Identifying potential safety hazards associated with scientific equipment, materials, procedures, and settings

Safety in the science classroom and laboratory is of paramount importance to the science educator. The following is a general summary of the types of safety equipment that each school should have and the general locations where the protective equipment or devices should be maintained and used. Please note that this is only a partial list and that your school system should be reviewed for unique hazards and site-specific hazards.

The key to maintaining a safe learning environment is through proactive training and regular in-service updates for all staff and students who utilize the science laboratory. Proactive training should include how to identify potential hazards, evaluate potential hazards, and prevent or respond to hazards.

School systems should consider the following types of training:

- Right to Know (OSHA training on the importance and benefits of properly recognizing and safely working with hazardous materials)
- Basic chemical hygiene and training on how to read and understand a Material Safety Data Sheet
- Instruction on the use of fire extinguishers
- Instruction on the use of chemical fume hoods
- General guidance on when and how to use personal protective equipment (e.g. safety glasses and gloves)
- Instruction on how to monitor activities for potential impacts on indoor air quality

It is also important for the instructor to utilize **Material Data Safety Sheets**. You should maintain a copy of the Material Safety Data Sheet for every item in your chemical inventory. This information will assist you in determining how to store and handle materials by outlining the health and safety hazards posed by the substance. In most cases the manufacturer will provide recommendations with regard to protective equipment, ventilation, and storage practices. This information should be your first guide when considering the use of a new material or the use of a familiar material in a new way.

Frequent monitoring and in-service training on all equipment, materials, and procedures will help to ensure a safe and orderly laboratory environment. It will also provide everyone who uses the laboratory the safety fundamentals necessary to recognize a safety hazard and to respond appropriately.

Skill 17.4 Recognizing appropriate protocols for maintaining safety and for responding to emergencies during classroom laboratory activities

All science labs should contain the following **safety equipment**.
- Fire blanket that is visible and accessible
- Ground Fault Circuit Interrupters (GFCI) within two feet of water supplies
- Signs designating room exits
- Emergency shower providing a continuous flow of water
- Emergency eye wash station that can be activated by the foot or forearm
- Eye protection for every student
- A means of sanitizing equipment
- Emergency exhaust fans providing ventilation to the outside of the building
- Master cut-off switches for gas, electric, and compressed air; switches must have permanently attached handles; cut-off switches must be clearly labeled
- An ABC fire extinguisher
- Storage cabinets for flammable materials

- Chemical spill control kit
- Fume hood with a motor that is spark proof
- Protective laboratory aprons made of flame retardant material
- Signs that will alert of potential hazardous conditions
- Labeled containers for broken glassware, flammables, corrosives, and waste

Students should wear safety goggles when performing dissections, heating any item, or using acids and bases. Hair should always be tied back and objects should never be placed in the mouth. Food should not be consumed while in the laboratory. Hands should always be washed before and after laboratory experiments. In case of an accident, eye washes and showers should be used for eye contamination or a chemical spill that covers the student's body. Small chemical spills should only be contained and cleaned by the teacher. Kitty litter or a chemical spill kit should be used to clean a spill. For large spills, the school administration and the local fire department should be notified. Biological spills should only be handled by the teacher. Contamination with biological waste can be cleaned by using bleach when appropriate. Accidents and injuries should always be reported to the school administration and local health facilities. The severity of the accident or injury will determine the course of action.

It is the responsibility of the teacher to provide a safe environment for his or her students. Proper supervision greatly reduces the risk of injury and a teacher should never leave a class for any reason without providing alternate supervision. After an accident, two factors are considered: **foreseeability** and **negligence**. Foreseeability is the anticipation that an event may occur under certain circumstances. Negligence is the failure to exercise ordinary or reasonable care. Safety procedures should be a part of the science curriculum, and a well managed classroom is important to avoid potential lawsuits.

Skill 17.5 Demonstrating knowledge of the role of models in science

The model is a basic element of the scientific method. Many things in science are studied with models. A model is any simplification or substitute for what we are actually studying. A model is a substitute, but it is similar to what it represents. We encounter models regularly in all areas of science. For example, The Periodic Table of the Elements is a model chemists use for predicting the properties of the elements. Physicists use Newton's laws to predict how objects will interact, such as planets and spaceships. In geology, the continental drift model predicts the past positions of continents. Samples, ideas, and methods are all examples of models. The primary activity of the hundreds of thousands of US scientists is to produce new models, resulting in the publication of tens of thousands of scientific papers every year.

Types of models:

- Scale models: models that are downsized or enlarged copies of their target systems such as classroom models of proteins, DNA, etc.
- Idealized models: an idealization is a deliberate simplification of something complicated with the objective of making it easier to understand. Some examples are frictionless planes, point masses, and isolated systems.
- Analogical models: standard examples of analogical models are the billiard ball model of a gas, the computer model of the mind, or the liquid drop model of the nucleus.
- Phenomenological models: these are models that are independent of theories.
- Data models: these are corrected, rectified, regimented, and–in many instances–idealized versions of the data we gain from immediate observation (raw data).
- Theory models: any structure is a model if it represents an idea (theory). An example of this is a flow chart, which summarizes a set of ideas.

Uses of models:

1. Models are crucial for understanding the structure and function of processes in science
2. Models help us visualize the organs or systems they represent, just like putting a face to a person
3. Models are very useful to predict and foresee future events like hurricanes

Limitations:

1. Though models are very useful to us, they can never replace the real thing
2. Models are not exactly like the real item they represent
3. We must exercise caution before presenting the models, as they may not be accurate
4. It is the responsibility of the educator to analyze the model critically for the proportions, content value, and other important data
5. One must be careful about the representation style; this style differs from person to person.

COMPETENCY 18.0   **UNDERSTAND THE SKILLS AND PROCEDURES FOR ANALYZING AND COMMUNICATING SCIENTIFIC DATA**

Skill 18.1 Recognizing the concepts of precision, accuracy, and error and identifying potential sources of error in gathering and recording data

Accuracy and precision

Accuracy is the degree of conformity of a measured, calculated quantity to its actual (true) value. Precision, also called reproducibility or repeatability, is the degree to which further measurements or calculations will show the same or similar results.

Accuracy is the degree of veracity while precision is the degree of reproducibility. The best analogy to explain accuracy and precision is the target comparison. Repeated measurements are compared to arrows that are fired at a target. Accuracy describes the closeness of arrows to the bullseye at the target center. Arrows that strike closer to the bullseye are considered more accurate. Precision, on the other hand, describes a cluster of arrows that land in the same location, distant from the target bullseye.

Systematic and random error

All experimental uncertainty is due to either random errors or systematic errors.

Random errors are statistical fluctuations in the measured data due to the precision limitations of the measurement device. Random errors usually result from the experimenter's inability to take repeatedly the same measurement in exactly the same way to get exactly the same value.

Systematic errors, by contrast, are reproducible inaccuracies that are consistently in the same direction. Systematic errors are often due to a problem, which persists throughout the entire experiment.

Systematic and random errors refer to problems associated with making measurements.

Mistakes made in the calculations or in reading the instrument are not considered in error analysis.

Skill 18.2 Applying appropriate mathematical concepts and computational skills to analyze data (e.g., using ratios; determining mean, median, and mode)

Modern science utilizes a number of other disciplines. Statistics is one such subject, and is essential for understanding science. Indeed, modern science would be impossible without modern statistics. Some common statistical terms are:

- Mean: The mathematical average of all the items. The mean is calculated by dividing the sum of a set of terms by the number of terms. This is also called the arithmetic mean or, more commonly, the "average".
- Median: The median depends on whether the number of terms is odd or even. If the number of terms is odd, then the median is the value of the term in the middle of the sorted set. Thus, the median value indicates there are an equal number of terms mathematically greater than and mathematically less than the value. If the number of terms is even, the median is the mean of the two terms in the middle of the sorted set.
- Mode: Mode is the value of the item that occurs with the highest frequency. Bimodal describes a situation where there are two terms with equal frequency.
- Range: Range is the difference between the maximum and minimum values of a data set. The range is the difference between two extreme points on the distribution curve.

Skill 18.3 Identifying methods (e.g., tables, graphs) and criteria for organizing data to aid in the analysis of data (e.g., detecting patterns)

The type of graphic representation used to display observations depends on the type of data collected. **Line graphs** compare different sets of related data and help predict future datum points. For example, a line graph could compare the rate of activity of different enzymes at varying temperatures. A **bar graph** or **histogram** compares different items and helps make comparisons based on the data. For example, a bar graph could compare the ages of children in a classroom. A **pie chart** is useful when organizing data as part of a whole. For example, a pie chart could display the percent of time students spend on various after school activities.

As previously noted, the researcher controls the independent variable. The independent variable usually is placed on the x-axis (horizontal axis). The dependent variable is influenced by the independent variable and is usually placed on the y-axis (vertical axis). It is important to choose the appropriate units for labeling the axes. It is often best to divide the largest value to be plotted by the number of blocks on the graph, and round to the nearest whole number.

Skill 18.4 Demonstrating knowledge of the use of data (e.g., tables, graphs) to support or challenge scientific arguments and claims

Scientists must communicate conclusions by clearly describing the information using accurate data, visual presentations, and other appropriate media such as a power point presentations. Examples of visual presentations are graphs (bar/line/pie), tables/charts, diagrams, and artwork. Scientists should use modern technology whenever necessary. The method of communication must be suitable to the audience. Written communication is as important as oral communication. The scientist's strongest ally is a solid set of reproducible data.

Skill 18.5 Identifying appropriate methods for communicating the outcomes of scientific investigations (e.g., presentations at science fairs, publication in peer-reviewed journals)

Because people often attempt to use scientific evidence in support of political or personal agendas, the ability to evaluate the credibility of scientific claims is a necessary skill in today's society. In evaluating scientific claims made in the media, public debates, and advertising, one should follow several guidelines.

First, scientific, peer-reviewed journals are the most accepted source for information on scientific experiments and studies. One should carefully scrutinize any claim that does not reference peer-reviewed literature.

Second, the media and those with an agenda to advance (e.g., advertisers and debaters) often overemphasize the certainty and importance of experimental results. One should question any scientific claim that sounds either too good to be true or overly certain.

Finally, knowledge of experimental design and the scientific method is important in evaluating the credibility of studies. For example, one should look for the inclusion of control groups and the presence of data to support the given conclusions.

Skill 18.6 Demonstrating familiarity with effective resources and strategies for reading to gain information about science-related topics and developing subject-area vocabulary

To facilitate independent learning in science, teachers must integrate content specific lessons with language and reading skills and activities. Learning science requires students to acquire and apply reading and writing strategies to new concepts in order to develop knowledge. The keys to developing subject-area vocabulary are the ability to write and an increased general vocabulary.

Writing is an important step in the development of science knowledge. In gathering information students learn to take notes in a variety of methods, make outlines of readings (textual and support materials), and use various graphic organizers. When analyzing and synthesizing information students write summaries of main ideas, write lab reports, and learn to keep journals. Written reports, web sites, projects, and multimedia presentations are created to demonstrate knowledge and understanding.

The next step in increasing scientific knowledge is subject area vocabulary development. Such development allows students to communicate in science courses and understand subject-area specific terminology. Science vocabulary may be taught explicitly or in the context of scientific readings. Explicit vocabulary instruction is easily accomplished through vocabulary lessons, drill and memorization. Teaching vocabulary in the context of scientific readings will require students to draw on their own schema, deductively understanding new words and concepts. To support both of these methods of vocabulary instruction, teachers should provide frequent opportunities for students to use subject-area vocabulary in their reading, writing, and speaking.

The National Science Teachers Association reviews and recommends books, materials, and technologies that offer strategies assisting teachers in the development of subject-area vocabulary. NSTA publications, grade-specific journals, and online resources support teachers with recent studies, best practices, and the opportunity for collaboration with other science educators.

Sample Exam

Directions: Read each item and select the best response.

1. **Bacteria commonly reproduce by a process called binary fission. Which of the following best defines this process?**
   (Rigorous) (Skill 1.1)

   A. viral vectors carry DNA to new bacteria

   B. DNA from one bacterium enters another

   C. DNA doubles and the bacterial cell divides

   D. DNA from dead cells is absorbed into bacteria

2. **Protists are classified into major groups according to...**
   (Rigorous) (Skill 1.1)

   A. their method of obtaining nutrition.

   B. reproduction.

   C. metabolism.

   D. their form and function.

3. **In comparison to protist cells, moneran cells...**
   (Rigorous) (Skill 1.1)

   I. are usually smaller.
   II. evolved later.
   III. are more complex.
   IV. contain more organelles.

   A. I

   B. I and II

   C. II and III

   D. I and IV

4. **The Endosymbiotic theory states that...**
   (Rigorous) (Skill 1.1)

   A. eukaryotes arose from prokaryotes.

   B. animals evolved in close relationships with one another.

   C. the prokaryotes arose from eukaryotes.

   D. life arose from inorganic compounds.

5. The shape of a cell depends on its...
(Easy) (Skill 1.1)

A. function.

B. structure.

C. age.

D. size.

6. Thermoacidophiles are...
(Rigorous) (Skill 1.1)

A. prokaryotes.

B. eukaryotes.

C. bacteria.

D. archaea.

7. Which of the following is not a type of fiber that makes up the cytoskeleton?
(Average Rigor) (Skill 1.1)

A. vacuoles

B. microfilaments

C. microtubules

D. intermediate filaments

8. Water movement to the top of a twenty foot tree is most likely due to which principle?
(Rigorous) (Skill 1.4)

A. osmostic pressure

B. xylem pressure

C. capillarity

D. transpiration

9. Which of the following are properties of water?
(Rigorous) (Skill 2.1)

I. High specific heat
II. Strong ionic bonds
III. Good solvent
IV. High freezing point

A. I, III, IV

B. II and III

C. I and II

D. II, III, IV

10. The loss of an electron is _____ and the gain of an electron is _____.
(Rigorous) (Skill 2.2)

A. oxidation, reduction

B. reduction, oxidation

C. glycolysis, photosynthesis

D. photosynthesis, glycolysis

11. **The product of anaerobic respiration in animals is...**
(Average Rigor) (Skill 2.2)

   A. carbon dioxide.

   B. lactic acid.

   C. pyruvate.

   D. ethyl alcohol

12. **Carbon dioxide is fixed in the form of glucose in...**
(Rigorous) (Skill 2.2)

   A. the Krebs cycle.

   B. the light reactions.

   C. the dark reactions (Calvin cycle).

   D. glycolysis.

13. **During the Krebs cycle, 8 carrier molecules are formed. What are they?**
(Rigorous) (Skill 2.2)

   A. 3 NADH, 3 FADH, 2 ATP

   B. 6 NADH and 2 ATP

   C. 4 $FADH_2$ and 4 ATP

   D. 6 NADH and 2 $FADH_2$

14. **In the electron transport chain, all the following are true except...**
(Rigorous) (Skill 2.2)

   A. it occurs in the mitochondrion.

   B. it does not make ATP directly.

   C. the net gain of energy is 30 ATP.

   D. most molecules in the electron transport chain are proteins.

15. **The most ATP is generated through...**
(Average Rigor) (Skill 2.2)

   A. fermentation.

   B. glycolysis.

   C. chemiosmosis.

   D. the Krebs cycle.

16. **Which does not affect enzyme rate?**
(Rigorous) (Skill 2.3)

   A. increase of temperature

   B. amount of substrate

   C. pH

   D. size of the cell

17. **Which of the following is a monomer?**
    (Rigorous) (Skill 2.4)

    A. RNA

    B. glycogen

    C. DNA

    D. amino acid

18. **A type of molecule not found in the membrane of an animal cell is...**
    (Rigorous) (Skill 2.4)

    A. phospholipid.

    B. protein.

    C. cellulose.

    D. cholesterol.

19. **The area of a DNA nucleotide that varies is the...**
    (Rigorous) (Skill 2.4)

    A. deoxyribose.

    B. phosphate group.

    C. nitrogenous base.

    D. sugar.

20. **In DNA, adenine bonds with _____, while cytosine bonds with _____.**
    (Average Rigor) (Skill 2.4)

    A. thymine/guanine

    B. adenine/cytosine

    C. cytosine/adenine

    D. guanine/thymine

21. **Which protein structure consists of the coils and folds of polypeptide chains?**
    (Rigorous) (Skill 2.4)

    A. secondary structure

    B. quaternary structure

    C. tertiary structure

    D. primary structure

22. **In the comparison of respiration to photosynthesis, which statement is true?**
    (Rigorous) (Skill 3.2)

    A. oxygen is a waste product in photosynthesis but not in respiration

    B. glucose is produced in respiration but not in photosynthesis

    C. carbon dioxide is formed in photosynthesis but not in respiration

    D. water is formed in respiration but not in photosynthesis

23. **Oxygen is given off in the...**
    (Rigorous) (Skill 3.2)

    A. light reactions of photosynthesis.

    B. dark reactions of photosynthesis.

    C. Krebs cycle.

    D. reduction of NAD+ to NADH.

24. **A muscular adaptation to move food through the digestive system is called...**
    (Average Rigor) (Skill 3.2)

    A. peristalsis.

    B. passive transport.

    C. voluntary action.

    D. bulk transport.

25. **Which photosystem makes ATP?**
    (Rigorous) (Skill 3.2)

    A. photosystem I

    B. photosystem II

    C. photosystem III

    D. photosystem IV

26. **Which is an example of the use of energy to move a substance through a membrane from areas of low concentration to areas of high concentration?**
    (Average Rigor) (Skill 3.3)

    A. osmosis

    B. active transport

    C. exocytosis

    D. phagocytosis

27. **A plant cell is placed in salt water. The resulting movement of water out of the cell is called...**
    (Average Rigor) (Skill 3.3)

    A. facilitated diffusion.

    B. diffusion.

    C. transpiration.

    D. osmosis.

28. **According to the fluid-mosaic model of the cell membrane, membranes are composed of...**
    (Rigorous) (Skill 3.3)

    A. phospholipid bilayers with proteins embedded in the layers.

    B. one layer of phospholipids with cholesterol embedded in the layer.

    C. two layers of protein with lipids embedded in the layers.

    D. DNA and fluid proteins.

29. **This stage of mitosis includes cytokinesis or division of the cytoplasm and its organelles.**
(Rigorous) (Skill 4.1)

A. anaphase

B. interphase

C. prophase

D. telophase

30. **Replication of chromosomes occurs during which phase of the cell cycle?**
(Average Rigor) (Skill 4.1)

A. prophase

B. interphase

C. metaphase

D. anaphase

31. **Which statement regarding mitosis is correct?**
(Average Rigor) (Skill 4.1)

A. diploid cells produce haploid cells for sexual reproduction

B. sperm and egg cells are produced

C. diploid cells produce diploid cells for growth and repair

D. it allows for greater genetic diversity

32. **In a plant cell, telophase is described as...**
(Average Rigor) (Skill 4.1)

A. the time of chromosome doubling.

B. cell plate formation.

C. the time when crossing over occurs.

D. cleavage furrow formation.

33. **Identify this stage of mitosis.**
(Average Rigor) (Skill 4.1)

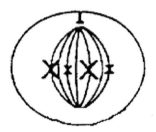

A. anaphase

B. metaphase

C. telophase

D. prophase

34. Identify this stage of mitosis.
(Average Rigor) (Skill 4.1)

A. prophase

B. telophase

C. anaphase

D. metaphase

35. Identify this stage of mitosis.
(Average Rigor) (Skill 4.1)

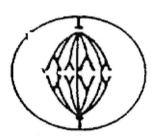

A. anaphase

B. metaphase

C. prophase

D. telophase

36. Which process(es) result(s) in a haploid chromosome number?
(Average Rigor) (Skill 4.1)

A. both meiosis and mitosis

B. mitosis

C. meiosis

D. replication and division

37. Which term is not associated with the water cycle?
(Easy) (Skill 4.1)

A. precipitation

B. transpiration

C. fixation

D. evaporation

38. Which process contributes to the large variety of living things in the world today?
(Average Rigor) (Skill 4.1)

A. meiosis

B. asexual reproduction

C. mitosis

D. alternation of generations

39. **Genes function in specifying the structure of which molecule?**
    (Easy) (Skill 4.3)

    A. carbohydrates

    B. lipids

    C. nucleic acids

    D. proteins

40. **Segments of DNA can be transferred from the DNA of one organism to another through the use of which of the following?**
    (Average Rigor) (Skill 4.1)

    A. bacterial plasmids

    B. viruses

    C. chromosomes from frogs

    D. plant DNA

41. **A virus that can remain dormant until a certain environmental condition causes its rapid increase is said to be...**
    (Average Rigor) (Skill 4.4)

    A. lytic.

    B. benign.

    C. saprophytic.

    D. lysogenic.

42. **Homozygous individuals...**
    (Rigorous) (Skill 5.1)

    A. have two different alleles.

    B. are of the same species.

    C. have the same features.

    D. have a pair of identical alleles.

43. **The Law of Segregation defined by Mendel states that...**
    (Rigorous) (Skill 5.1)

    A. when sex cells form, the two alleles that determine a trait will end up on different gametes.

    B. only one of two alleles is expressed in a heterozygous organism.

    C. the allele expressed is the dominant allele.

    D. alleles of one trait do not affect the inheritance of alleles on another chromosome.

44. **When a white flower is crossed with a red flower, incomplete dominance can be seen by the production of which of the following?**
    (Average Rigor) (Skill 5.1)

    A. pink flowers

    B. red flowers

    C. white flowers

    D. red and white flowers

45. A child with type O blood has a father with type A blood and a mother with type B blood. The genotypes of the parents respectively would be which of the following?
(Average Rigor) (Skill 5.1)

A. AA and BO

B. AO and BO

C. AA and BB

D. AO and OO

46. All the following statements regarding both a mitochondria and a chloroplast are correct except...
(Rigorous) (Skill 5.3)

A. they both produce energy over a gradient.

B. they both have DNA and are capable of reproduction.

C. they both transform light energy to chemical energy.

D. they both make ATP.

47. Crossing over, which increases genetic diversity occurs during which stage(s)?
(Average Rigor) (Skill 5.3)

A. telophase II in meiosis

B. metaphase in mitosis

C. interphase in both mitosis and meiosis

D. prophase I in meiosis

48. Which of the following is not posttranscriptional processing?
(Rigorous) (Skill 6.2)

A. 5' capping

B. intron splicing

C. polypeptide splicing

D. 3' polyadenylation

49. What is the correct order of steps in protein synthesis?
(Easy) (Skill 6.2)

A. transcription, then replication

B. transcription, then translation

C. translation, then transcription

D. replication, then translation

50. This carries amino acids to the ribosome in protein synthesis.
(Easy) (Skill 6.2)

A. messenger RNA

B. ribosomal RNA

C. transfer RNA

D. DNA

51. A DNA molecule has the sequence of ACTATG. What is the anticodon of this molecule?
     (Easy) (Skill 6.2)

     A. UGAUAC

     B. ACUAUG

     C. TGATAC

     D. ACTATG

52. DNA synthesis results in a strand that is synthesized continuously. This is the...
     (Average Rigor) (Skill 6.2)

     A. lagging strand.

     B. leading strand.

     C. template strand.

     D. complementary strand.

53. Evolution occurs in...
     (Average Rigor) (Skill 6.4)

     A. individuals.

     B. populations.

     C. organ systems.

     D. cells.

54. Which type of cell would contain the most mitochondria?
     (Rigorous) (Skill 6.5)

     A. muscle cell

     B. nerve cell

     C. epithelium

     D. blood cell

55. The polymerase chain reaction...
     (Rigorous) (Skill 6.6)

     A. is a group of polymerases.

     B. is a technique for amplifying DNA.

     C. is a primer for DNA synthesis.

     D. is synthesis of polymerase.

56. Any change that affects the sequence of bases in a gene is called a(n)...
     (Average Rigor) (Skill 6.6)

     A. deletion.

     B. polyploid.

     C. mutation.

     D. duplication.

57. **Which of the following is not true regarding restriction enzymes?**
(Rigorous) (Skill 6.6)

A. they do not aid in recombination procedures

B. they are used in genetic engineering

C. they are named after the bacteria in which they naturally occur

D. they identify and splice certain base sequences on DNA

58. **A genetic engineering advancement in the medical field is...**
(Easy) (Skill 6.7)

A. gene therapy.

B. pesticides.

C. degradation of harmful chemicals.

D. antibiotics.

59. **Given the choice of lab activities, which would you omit?**
(Easy) (Skill 6.8)

A. a genetics experiment tracking the fur color of mice

B. dissecting a preserved fetal pig

C. a lab relating temperature to respiration rate using live goldfish

D. pithing a frog to see the action of circulation

60. **Man's scientific name is *Homo sapiens*. Choose the proper classification beginning with kingdom and ending with order.**
(Average Rigor) (Skill 7.1)

A. Animalia, Vertebrata, Mammalia, Primate, Hominidae

B. Animalia, Vertebrata, Chordata, Mammalia, Primate

C. Animalia, Chordata, Vertebrata, Mammalia, Primate

D. Chordata, Vertebrata, Primate, Homo, sapiens

61. **The scientific name *Canis familiaris* refers to the animal's...**
(Average Rigor) (Skill 7.1)

A. kingdom and phylum names

B. genus and species names

C. class and species names

D. order and family names

62. **Members of the same species...**
(Average Rigor) (Skill 7.1)

A. look identical.

B. never change.

C. reproduce successfully within their group.

D. live in the same geographic location.

63. **Which phylum accounts for 85% of all animal species?**
    (Average Rigor) (Skill 7.1)

    A. Nematoda

    B. Chordata

    C. Arthropoda

    D. Cnidaria

64. **The wing of a bird, human arm, and whale flipper have the same bone structure. These are called...**
    (Average Rigor) (Skill 7.1)

    A. polymorphic structures.

    B. homologous structures.

    C. vestigial structures.

    D. analogous structures.

65. **Which kingdom is comprised of organisms made of one cell with no nuclear membrane?**
    (Rigorous) (Skill 7.3)

    A. Monera

    B. Protista

    C. Fungi

    D. Algae

66. **All of the following are members of the Kingdom Fungi except...**
    (Average Rigor) (Skill 7.3)

    A. mold.

    B. algae.

    C. mildew.

    D. mushrooms.

67. **The two major ways to determine taxonomic classification are...**
    (Rigorous) (Skill 7.4)

    A. evolution and phylogeny.

    B. reproductive success and evolution.

    C. phylogeny and morphology.

    D. size and color.

68. **The term "phenotype" refers to which of the following?**
    (Easy) (Skill 8.3)

    A. a condition which is heterozygous

       B. the genetic makeup of an individual

    C. a condition which is homozygous

    D. how the genotype is expressed

69. **The biological species concept applies to...**
    (Easy) (Skill 8.5)

    A. asexual organisms.

    B. extinct organisms.

    C. sexual organisms.

    D. fossil organisms.

70. **Spores are the reproduction mode for which of the following group of plants?**
    (Rigorous) (Skill 9.1)

    A. algae

    B. flowering plants

    C. conifers

    D. ferns

71. **Which is the correct sequence of embryonic development in a frog?**
    (Average Rigor) (Skill 9.2)

    A. cleavage – blastula – gastrula

    B. cleavage – gastrula – blastula

    C. blastula – cleavage – gastrula

    D. gastrula – blastula – cleavage

72. **Which of the following is the correct order of the stages of plant development from egg to adult plant?**
    (Rigorous) (Skill 9.4)

    A. morphogenesis, growth, and cellular differentiation

    B. cell differentiation, growth, and morphogenesis

    C. growth, morphogenesis, and cellular differentiation

    D. growth, cellular differentiation, and morphogenesis

73. **The process in which pollen grains are released from the anthers is called...**
    (Easy) (Skill 9.4)

    A. pollination.

    B. fertilization.

    C. blooming.

    D. dispersal.

74. **Which of the following is not a characteristic of a monocot?**
    (Rigorous) (Skill 9.4)

    A. parallel veins in leaves

    B. petals of flowers occur in multiples of 4 or 5

    C. one seed leaf

    D. vascular tissue scattered throughout the stem

75. **How are angiosperms different from other groups of plants?**
(Average Rigor) (Skill 9.4)

A. presence of flowers and fruits

B. production of spores for reproduction

C. true roots and stems

D. seed production

76. **Generations of plants alternate between...**
(Rigorous) (Skill 9.4)

A. angiosperms and bryophytes.

B. flowering and nonflowering stages.

C. seed bearing and spore bearing plants.

D. haploid and diploid stages.

77. **Double fertilization refers to which choice of the following?**
(Average Rigor) (Skill 9.4)

A. two sperm fertilizing one egg

B. fertilization of a plant by gametes from two separate plants

C. two sperm enter the plant embryo sac; one sperm fertilizes the egg, the other forms the endosperm

D. the production of non-identical twins through fertilization of two separate eggs

78. **What is necessary for diffusion to occur?**
(Average Rigor) (Skill 10.1)

A. carrier proteins

B. energy

C. a concentration gradient

D. a membrane

79. **As the amount of waste production increases in a cell, the rate of excretion...**
(Rigorous) (Skill 10.1)

A. slowly decreases.

B. remains the same.

C. increases.

D. stops due to cell death.

80. **Identify the correct sequence of organization of living things.**
(Rigorous) (Skill 10.2)

A. cell – organelle – organ – tissue – organ system – organism

B. cell – tissue – organ – organelle – organ system – organism

C. organelle – cell – tissue – organ – organ system – organism

D. organ system – tissue – organelle – cell – organism – organ

81. **Which is not a characteristic of living things?**
    (Rigorous) (Skill 10.3)

    A. movement

    B. cellular structure

    C. metabolism

    D. reproduction

82. **Which is the correct statement regarding the human nervous system and the human endocrine system?**
    (Average Rigor) (Skill 10.3)

    A. the nervous system maintains homeostasis whereas the endocrine system does not

    B. endocrine glands produce neurotransmitters whereas nerves produce hormones

    C. nerve signals travel on neurons whereas hormones travel through the blood

    D. the nervous system involves chemical transmission whereas the endocrine system does not

83. **In angiosperms, the food for the developing plant is found in which of the following structures?**
    (Rigorous) (Skill 10.4)

    A. ovule

    B. endosperm

    C. male gametophyte

    D. cotyledon

84. **If the niches of two species overlap, what usually results?**
    (Average Rigor) (Skill 10.4)

    A. a symbiotic relationship

    B. cooperation

    C. competition

    D. a new species

85. **Oxygen created in photosynthesis comes from the breakdown of...**
    (Easy) (Skill 10.4)

    A. carbon dioxide.

    B. water.

    C. glucose.

    D. carbon monoxide.

86. **The first cells that evolved on earth were probably of which type?**
(Rigorous) (Skill 11.1)

A. autotrophs

B. eukaryotes

C. heterotrophs

D. prokaryotes

87. **What controls gas exchange on the bottom of a plant leaf?**
(Average Rigor) (Skill 11.3)

A. stomata

B. epidermis

C. collenchyma and schlerenchyma

D. palisade mesophyll

88. **All of the following are found in the dermis layer of skin except...**
(Easy) (Skill 11.3)

A. sweat glands.

B. keratin.

C. hair follicles.

D. blood vessels.

89. **The role of neurotransmitters in nerve action is...**
(Easy) (Skill 12.1)

A. to turn off the sodium pump.

B. to turn off the calcium pump.

C. to send impulses to neurons.

D. to send impulses to the body.

90. **Fats are broken down by which substance?**
(Rigorous) (Skill 12.1)

A. bile produced in the gall bladder

B. lipase produced in the gall bladder

C. glucagons produced in the liver

D. bile produced in the liver

91. **Fertilization in humans usually occurs in the...**
(Easy) (Skill 12.1)

A. uterus.

B. ovary.

C. fallopian tubes.

D. vagina.

92. Food is carried through the digestive tract by a series of wave-like contractions. This process is called...
(Easy) (Skill 12.1)

A. peristalsis.

B. chyme.

C. digestion.

D. absorption.

93. Movement is possible by the action of muscles pulling on...
(Easy) (Skill 12.1)

A. skin.

B. bones.

C. joints.

D. ligaments.

94. All of the following are functions of the skin except...
(Easy) (Skill 12.1)

A. storage.

B. protection.

C. sensation.

D. regulation of temperature.

95. A school age boy had the chicken pox as a baby. He will most likely not get this disease again because of...
(Average) (Skill 12.1)

A. passive immunity.

B. vaccination.

C. antibiotics.

D. active immunity.

96. Hormones are essential to the regulation of reproduction. What organ is responsible for the release of hormones for sexual maturity?
(Average) (Skill 12.2)

A. pituitary gland

B. hypothalamus

C. pancreas

D. thyroid gland

97. All of the following are density independent factors that affect a population except...
(Average Rigor) (Skill 13.5)

A. temperature.

B. rainfall.

C. predation.

D. soil nutrients.

98. A clownfish is protected by the sea anemone's tentacles. In turn, the anemone receives uneaten food from the clownfish. This is an example of...
(Easy) (Skill 13.5)

A. mutualism.

B. parasitism.

C. commensalism.

D. competition.

99. High humidity and temperature stability are present in which of the following biomes?
(Average Rigor) (Skill 14.1)

A. taiga

B. deciduous forest

C. desert

D. tropical rain forest

100. Which of the following is not an abiotic factor?
(Rigorous) (Skill 14.1)

A. temperature

B. rainfall

C. soil quality

D. bacteria

101. If DDT were present in an ecosystem, which of the following organisms would have the highest concentration in its system?
(Average Rigor) (Skill 14.3)

A. grasshopper

B. eagle

C. frog

D. crabgrass

102. Which trophic level has the highest ecological efficiency?
(Rigorous) (Skill 15.1)

A. decomposers

B. producers

C. tertiary consumers

D. secondary consumers

103. Primary succession occurs after...
(Rigorous) (Skill 15.5)

A. nutrient enrichment.

B. a forest fire.

C. bare rock is exposed after a water table recedes.

D. a housing development is built.

104. Which biome is the most prevalent on Earth?
(Rigorous) (Skill 14.1)

A. marine

B. desert

C. savanna

D. tundra

105. A student designed a science project testing the effects of light and water on plant growth. You would recommend that she...
(Average Rigor) (Skill 16.1)

A. manipulate the temperature as well.

B. also alter the pH of the water as another variable.

C. omit either water or light as a variable.

D. also alter the light concentration as another variable.

106. A scientific theory...
(Average) (Skill 16.2)

A. proves scientific accuracy.

B. is never rejected.

C. results in a medical breakthrough.

D. may be altered at a later time.

107. Which is the correct order of methodology? 1) testing revised explanation, 2) setting up a controlled experiment to test an explanation, 3) drawing a conclusion, 4) suggesting an explanation for observations, and 5) comparing observed results to hypothesized results
(Average Rigor) (Skill 16.3)

A. 4, 2, 3, 1, 5

B. 3, 1, 4, 2, 5

C. 4, 2, 5, 1, 3

D. 2, 5, 4, 1, 3

108. Identify the control in the following experiment. A student grew four plants under the following conditions and was measuring photosynthetic rate by measuring mass. 2 plants in 50% light and 2 plants in 100% light.
(Average Rigor) (Skill 16.5)

A. plants grown with no added nutrients

B. plants grown in the dark

C plants in 100% light

D. plants in 50% light

109. In an experiment measuring the growth of bacteria at different temperatures, identify the independent variable.
(Average Rigor) (*Skill 16.5*)

A. growth of number of colonies

B. temperature

C. type of bacteria used

D. light intensity

110. Biological waste should be disposed of...
(Easy) (*Skill 17.1*)

A. in the trash can.

B. under a fume hood.

C. in the broken glass box.

D. in an autoclavable biohazard bag.

111. Chemicals should be stored...
(Easy) (*Skill 17.1*)

A. in a cool dark room.

B. in a dark room.

C. according to their reactivity with other substances.

D. in a double locked room.

112. The "Right to Know" law states...
(Rigorous) (*Skill 17.1*)

A. the inventory of toxic chemicals checked against the "Substance List" be available.

B. that students are to be informed of alternatives to dissection.

C. that science teachers are to be informed of student allergies.

D. that students are to be informed of infectious microorganisms used in lab.

113. A light microscope has an ocular of 10X and an objective of 40X. What is the total magnification?
(Easy) (*Skill 17.1*)

A. 400X

B. 30X

C. 50X

D. 4000X

114. Electrophoresis separates DNA on the basis of...
(Rigorous) (*Skill 17.1*)

A. amount of current.

B. molecular size.

C. positive charge of the molecule.

D. solubility of the gel.

115. Which is not a correct statement regarding the use of a light microscope?
(Easy) (Skill 17.1)

A. carry the microscope with two hands

B. store on the low power objective

C. clean all lenses with lens paper

D. Focus first on high power

116. Spectrophotometry utilizes the principle of...
(Easy) (Skill 17.1)

A. light transmission.

B. molecular weight.

C. solubility of the substance.

D. electrical charges.

117. Chromotography is most often associated with the separation of...
(Rigorous) (Skill 17.1)

A. nutritional elements.

B. DNA.

C. proteins.

D. plant pigments.

118. The reading of a meniscus in a graduated cylinder is done at the...
(Easy) (Skill 17.1)

A. top of the meniscus.

B. middle of the meniscus.

C. bottom of the meniscus.

D. closest whole number.

119. Which item should always be used when using chemicals with noxious vapors?
(Easy) (Skill 17.3)

A. eye protection

B. face shield

C. fume hood

D. lab apron

120. Who should be notified in the case of a serious chemical spill?
(Easy)(Skill 17.4)

I. the custodian
II. the fire department
III. the chemistry teacher
IV. the administration

A. I

B. II

C. II and III

D. II and IV

121. **In which situation would a science teacher be liable?**
     (Average Rigor) (Skill 17.4)

     A. a teacher leaves to receive an emergency phone call and a student slips and falls

     B. a student removes their goggles and gets dissection fluid in their eye

     C. a faulty gas line results in a fire

     D. a students cuts themselves with a scalpel

122. **Which statement best defines negligence?**
     (Average Rigor) (Skill 17.4)

     A. failure to give oral instructions for those with reading disabilities

     B. failure to exercise ordinary care

     C. inability to supervise a large group of students

     D. reasonable anticipation that an event may occur

Answer Key

1. C	32. B	63. C	94. A
2. D	33. B	64. B	95. D
3. A	34. B	65. A	96. B
4. A	35. A	66. B	97. C
5. A	36. C	67. C	98. A
6. D	37. C	68. D	99. D
7. A	38. A	69. C	100. D
8. D	39. D	70. D	101. B
9. A	40. A	71. A	102. B
10. A	41. D	72. C	103. C
11. B	42. D	73. A	104. C
12. C	43. A	74. B	105. A
13. D	44. A	75. A	106. D
14. C	45. B	76. D	107. C
15. C	46. C	77. C	108. C
16. D	47. D	78. C	109. B
17. D	48. C	79. C	110. D
18. C	49. B	80. C	111. C
19. C	50. C	81. A	112. A
20. A	51. B	82. C	113. A
21. A	52. B	83. B	114. B
22. A	53. B	84. C	115. D
23. A	54. A	85. B	116. A
24. A	55. B	86. D	117. D
25. A	56. C	87. A	118. C
26. B	57. A	88. B	119. C
27. D	58. A	89. A	120. D
28. A	59. D	90. D	121. A
29. D	60. C	91. C	122. B
30. B	61. B	92. A	
31. C	62. C	93. B	

Rigor Table

	Easy %20	Average Rigor %40	Rigorous %40
Question #	5,37,39,49,50,51,58,59 68,69,73,85,88,89,91,92 93,94,98,110,111,113,115, 116,118,119,120	7,11,15,20,24,26,27,30, 31,32,33,34,35,36,38,40 41,44,45,47,52,53,56,60 61,62,63,64,66,71,75,77 78,82,84,87,95,97,99,101, 105,106,107,108,109,121, 122	1,2,3,4,6,8,9,10,12,13, 14,16,17,18,19,21,22, 23,25,28,29,42,43,46, 48,54,55,57,65,67,70 72,74,75,79,80,81,83 8690,100,102,103,104, 112,114,117

Rationales with Sample Questions

1. **Bacteria commonly reproduce by a process called binary fission. Which of the following best defines this process?**
    (Average Rigor) (Skill 4.4)

    A. viral vectors carry DNA to new bacteria
    B. DNA from one bacterium enters another
    C. DNA doubles and the bacterial cell divides
    D. DNA from dead cells is absorbed into bacteria

C. Binary fission is the asexual process in which the bacteria divide in half after the DNA doubles. This results in an exact clone of the parent cell.

2. **Protists are classified into major groups according to...**
    (Rigorous) (Skill 1.1)

    A. their method of obtaining nutrition.
    B. reproduction.
    C. metabolism.
    D. their form and function.

D. The chaotic status of names and concepts of the higher classification of the protists reflects their great diversity in form, function, and life styles. The protists are often grouped as algae (plant-like), protozoa (animal-like), or fungus-like based on the similarity of their lifestyle and characteristics to these more defined groups.

3. **In comparison to protist cells, moneran cells...**
    (Rigorous) (Skill 1.1)

    I. are usually smaller
    II. evolved later
    III. are more complex
    IV. contain more organelles

    A. I
    B. I and II
    C. II and III
    D. I and IV

A. Moneran cells are almost always smaller than protists. Moneran cells are prokaryotic; therefore, they are less complex and have no organelles. Prokaryotes were the first cells on Earth and therefore evolved before the eukaryotic protists.

4.   **The Endosymbiotic theory states that...**
      (Rigorous) (Skill 1.1)

    A. eukaryotes arose from prokaryotes.
    B. animals evolved in close relationships with one another.
    C. prokaryotes arose from eukaryotes.
    D. life arose from inorganic compounds.

A. The Endosymbiotic theory of the origin of eukaryotes states that eukaryotes arose from symbiotic groups of prokaryotic cells. According to this theory, smaller prokaryotes lived within larger prokaryotic cells, eventually evolving into chloroplasts and mitochondria.

5.   **The shape of a cell depends on its...**
      (Easy) (Skill 1.1)

    A. function.
    B. structure.
    C. age.
    D. size.

A. In most living organisms, cellular structure is based on function.

6.   **Thermoacidophiles are...**
      (Rigorous) (Skill 1.1)

    A. prokaryotes.
    B. eukaryotes.
    C. protists.
    D. archaea.

D. Thermoacidophiles, methanogens, and halobacteria are members of the archaea group. They are as different from prokaryotes as prokaryotes are from eukaryotes.

7.   **Which of the following is not a type of fiber that makes up the cytoskeleton?**
      (Average Rigor) (Skill 1.1)

    A. vacuoles
    B. microfilaments
    C. microtubules
    D. intermediate filaments

A. Vacuoles are mostly found in plants and hold stored food and pigments. The other three choices are fibers that make up the cytoskeleton found in both plant and animal cells.

8.   **Water movement to the top of a twenty foot tree is most likely due to which principle?**
       (Rigorous) (Skill 1.4)

    A. osmostic pressure
    B. xylem pressure
    C. capillarity
    D. transpiration

D. Xylem is the tissue that transports water upward. Transpiration is the force that pulls the water upwards. Transpiration is the evaporation of water from leaves.

9.   **Which of the following are properties of water?**
       (Rigorous) (Skill 2.1)

    I. **High specific heat**
    II. **Strong ionic bonds**
    III. **Good solvent**
    IV. **High freezing point**

    A. I, III, IV
    B. II and III
    C. I and II
    D. II, III, IV

A. All are properties of water except strong ionic bonds. Water is held together by polar covalent bonds between hydrogen and oxygen.

10.   **The loss of an electron is _____ and the gain of an electron is**

       _____.
       (Rigorous) (Skill 2.2)

    A. oxidation, reduction
    B. reduction, oxidation
    C. glycolysis, photosynthesis
    D. photosynthesis, glycolysis

A. Oxidation-reduction reactions are also known as redox reactions. In respiration, energy is released by the transfer of electrons by this process. The oxidation phase of this reaction involve the loss of an electron and the reduction phase involves the gain of an electron.

11.   **The product of anaerobic respiration in animals is...**
       (Average Rigor) (Skill 2.2)

    A. carbon dioxide.
    B. lactic acid.
    C. pyruvate.
    D. ethyl alcohol.

B. In anaerobic lactic acid fermentation, pyruvate is reduced by NADH to form lactic acid. This is the anaerobic process in animals. Alcoholic fermentation is the anaerobic process in yeast and some bacteria resulting in ethyl alcohol. Carbon dioxide and pyruvate are the products of aerobic respiration.

12.   **Carbon dioxide is fixed in the form of glucose in...**
       (Rigorous) (Skill 2.2)

    A. the Krebs cycle.
    B. the light reactions.
    C. the dark reactions (Calvin cycle).
    D. glycolysis.

C. The ATP produced during the light reaction is needed to convert carbon dioxide to glucose in the Calvin cycle.

13.   **During the Krebs cycle, 8 carrier molecules are formed. What are they?**
       (Rigorous) (Skill 2.2)

    A. 3 NADH, 3 FADH, 2 ATP
    B. 6 NADH and 2 ATP
    C. 4 $FADH_2$ and 4 ATP
    D. 6 NADH and 2 $FADH_2$

D. For each molecule of CoA that enters the Kreb's cycle, you get 3 NADH and 1 $FADH_2$. There are 2 molecules of CoA so the total yield is 6 NADH and 2 $FADH_2$ during the Krebs cycle.

14.   **In the electron transport chain, all the following are true except...**
       (Rigorous) (Skill 2.2)

    A. it occurs in the mitochondrion.
    B. it does not make ATP directly.
    C. the net gain of energy is 30 ATP.
    D. most molecules in the electron
       transport chain are proteins.

C. The end result of the electron transport chain is 34 molecules of ATP.

15.   **The most ATP is generated through...**
        (Average Rigor) (Skill 2.2)

   A. fermentation.
   B. glycolysis.
   C. chemiosmosis.
   D. the Krebs cycle.

C. The electron transport chain uses electrons to pump hydrogen ions across the mitochondrial membrane. This ion gradient is used to form ATP in a process called chemiosmosis. ATP is generated by the removal of hydrogen ions from NADH and $FADH_2$. This yields 34 ATP molecules.

16.   **Which does not affect enzyme rate?**
        (Rigorous) (Skill 2.3)

   A. increase of temperature
   B. amount of substrate
   C. pH
   D. size of the cell

D. Temperature and pH can affect the rate of reaction of an enzyme. The amount of substrate affects the enzyme as well. The enzyme acts on the substrate. The more substrate, the slower the enzyme rate. Therefore, the only choice left is D, the size of the cell, which has no effect on enzyme rate.

17.   **Which of the following is a monomer?**
        (Rigorous) (Skill 2.4)

   A. RNA
   B. glycogen
   C. DNA
   D. amino acid

D. A monomer is the simplest unit of structure for a particular macromolecule. Amino acids are the basic units that comprise a proteins. RNA and DNA are polymers consisting of nucleotides and glycogen is a polymer consisting of many molecules of glucose.

18.   **A type of molecule not found in the membrane of an animal cell is...**
        (Rigorous) (Skill 2.4)

    A. phospholipid.
    B. protein.
    C. cellulose.
    D. cholesterol.

C. Phospholipids, protein, and cholesterol are all found in animal cells. Cellulose, however, is only found in plant cells.

19.   **The area of a DNA nucleotide that varies is the...**
        (Rigorous) (Skill 2.4)

    A. deoxyribose.
    B. phosphate group.
    C. nitrogenous base.
    D. sugar.

C. DNA is made of a 5-carbon sugar (deoxyribose), a phosphate group, and a nitrogenous base. There are four nitrogenous bases in DNA that allow for the four different nucleotides.

20.   **In DNA, adenine bonds with _____, while cytosine bonds with _____.**
        (Average Rigor) (Skill 2.4)

    A. thymine/guanine
    B. adenine/cytosine
    C. cytosine/adenine
    D. guanine/thymine

A. In DNA, adenine pairs with thymine and cytosine pairs with guanine because of their nitrogenous base structures.

21. **Which protein structure consists of the coils and folds of polypeptide chains?**
     (Rigorous) (Skill 2.4)

     A. secondary structure
     B. quaternary structure
     C. tertiary structure
     D. primary structure

A. Primary structure is the protein's unique sequence of amino acids. Secondary structure is the coils and folds of polypeptide chains. The coils and folds are the result of hydrogen bonds along the polypeptide backbone. Tertiary structure is formed by bonding between the side chains of the amino acids. Quaternary structure is the overall structure of the protein from the aggregation of two or more polypeptide chain.

22. **In the comparison of respiration to photosynthesis, which statement is true?**
     (Rigorous) (Skill 3.2)

     A. oxygen is a waste product in photosynthesis but not in respiration
     B. glucose is produced in respiration but not in photosynthesis
     C. carbon dioxide is formed in photosynthesis but not in respiration
     D. water is formed in respiration but not in photosynthesis

A. In photosynthesis, water is split and the oxygen is given off as a waste product. In respiration, water and carbon dioxide are the waste products.

23. **Oxygen is given off in the...**
     (Rigorous) (Skill 3.2)

     A. light reactions of photosynthesis.
     B. dark reactions of photosynthesis.
     C. Krebs cycle.
     D. reduction of NAD+ to NADH.

A. The conversion of solar energy to chemical energy occurs in the light reactions. Electrons are transferred by the absorption of light by chlorophyll and cause water to split, releasing oxygen as a waste product.

24.   **A muscular adaptation to move food through the digestive system is called...**
       (Average Rigor) (Skill 3.2)

    A. peristalsis.
    B. passive transport.
    C. voluntary action.
    D. bulk transport.

A. Peristalsis is a process of wave-like contractions. This process allows food to be carried down the pharynx and though the digestive tract.

25.   **Which photosystem makes ATP?**
       (Rigorous) (Skill 3.2)

    A. photosystem I
    B. photosystem II
    C. photosystem III
    D. photosystem IV

A. Photosystem I is composed of a pair of chlorophyll *a* molecules It makes ATP whose energy is needed to build glucose.

26.   **Which is an example of the use of energy to move a substance through a membrane from areas of low concentration to areas of high concentration?**
       (Average Rigor) (Skill 3.3)

    A. osmosis
    B. active transport
    C. exocytosis
    D. phagocytosis

B. Active transport can move substances with or against the concentration gradient. This energy requiring process allows for molecules to move from areas of low concentration to areas of high concentration.

27.   A plant cell is placed in salt water. The resulting movement of water
       out of the cell is called...
       (Average Rigor) (Skill 3.3)

   A. facilitated diffusion.
   B. diffusion.
   C. transpiration.
   D. osmosis.

D. Osmosis is simply the diffusion of water across a semi-permeable membrane.
Water will diffuse out of the cell if there is less water on the outside of the cell.

28.   According to the fluid-mosaic model of the cell membrane, membranes
       are composed of...
       (Rigorous) (Skill 3.3)

   A. phospholipid bilayers with proteins embedded in the layers.
   B. one layer of phospholipids with cholesterol embedded in the layer.
   C. two layers of protein with lipids embedded the layers.
   D. DNA and fluid proteins.

A. Cell membranes are composed of two phospholipids with their hydrophobic tails
sandwiched between their hydrophilic heads, creating a lipid bilayer. The membrane
contains proteins embedded in the layer (integral proteins) and proteins on the surface
(peripheral proteins).

29.   This stage of mitosis includes cytokinesis or division of the cytoplasm and
       its organelles.
       (Rigorous) (Skill 4.1)

   A. anaphase
   B. interphase
   C. prophase
   D. telophase

D. The last stage of the mitotic phase is telophase. Here, the two nuclei form with a full
set of DNA each. The cell is pinched into two cells and cytokinesis, or division of the
cytoplasm and organelles, occurs.

30. **Replication of chromosomes occurs during which phase of the cell cycle?**
(Average Rigor) (Skill 4.1)

   A. prophase
   B. interphase
   C. metaphase
   D. anaphase

B. Interphase is the stage where the cell grows and copies the chromosomes in preparation for the mitotic phase.

31. **Which statement regarding mitosis is correct?**
(Average Rigor) (Skill 4.1)

   A. diploid cells produce haploid cells for sexual reproduction
   B. sperm and egg cells are produced
   C. diploid cells produce diploid cells for growth and repair
   D. it allows for greater genetic diversity

C. The purpose of mitotic cell division is to provide growth and repair in body (somatic) cells. The cells begin as diploid and produce diploid cells.

32. **In a plant cell, telophase is described as...**
(Average Rigor) (Skill 4.1)

   A. the time of chromosome doubling.
   B. cell plate formation.
   C. the time when crossing over occurs.
   D. cleavage furrow formation.

B. During plant cell telophase, a cell plate is observed whereas a cleavage furrow is formed in animal cells.

33.   Identify this stage of mitosis.
(Average Rigor) (Skill 4.1)

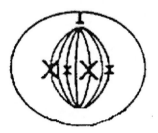

A. anaphase
B. metaphase
C. telophase
D. prophase

B. During metaphase, the centromeres are at opposite ends of the cell. Here the chromosomes are aligned with one another.

34.   Identify this stage of mitosis.
(Average Rigor) (Skill 4.1)

A. prophase
B. telophase
C. anaphase
D. metaphase

B. Telophase is the last stage of mitosis. Here, two nuclei become visible and the nuclear membrane reassembles.

35. **Identify this stage of mitosis.**
    (Average Rigor) (Skill 4.1)

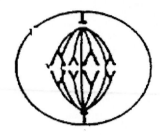

    A. anaphase
    B. metaphase
    C. prophase
    D. telophase

A. During anaphase, the centromeres split in half and homologous chromosomes separate.

36. **Which process(es) result(s) in a haploid chromosome number?**
    (Average Rigor) (Skill 4.1)

    A. both meiosis and mitosis
    B. mitosis
    C. meiosis
    D. replication and division

C. In meiosis, there are two consecutive cell divisions resulting in the reduction of the chromosome number by half (diploid to haploid).

37. **Which term is not associated with the water cycle?**
    (Easy) (Skill 4.1)

    A. precipitation
    B. transpiration
    C. fixation
    D. evaporation

C. Water is recycled through the processes of evaporation and precipitation. Transpiration is the evaporation of water from leaves. Fixation is not associated with the water cycle.

38. **Which process contributes to the large variety of living things in the world today?**
(Average Rigor) (Skill 4.1)

   A. meiosis
   B. asexual reproduction
   C. mitosis
   D. alternation of generations

A. During meiosis prophase I crossing over occurs. This exchange of genetic material between homologues increases diversity.

39. **Genes function in specifying the structure of which molecule?**
(Easy) (Skill 4.3)

   A. carbohydrates
   B. lipids
   C. nucleic acids
   D. proteins

D. Genes contain the sequence of nucleotides that code for amino acids. Amino acids are the building blocks of protein.

40. **Segments of DNA can be transferred from the DNA of one organism to another through the use of which of the following?**
(Average rigor) (Skill 4.1)

   A. bacterial plasmids
   B. viruses
   C. chromosomes from frogs
   D. plant DNA

A. Plasmids can transfer themselves (and therefore their genetic information) by a process called conjugation. This requires cell-to-cell contact.

41. **A virus that can remain dormant until a certain environmental condition causes its rapid increase is said to be...**
(Average rigor) (Skill 4.4)

   A. lytic.
   B. benign.
   C. saprophytic.
   D. lysogenic.

D. Lysogenic viruses remain dormant until something initiates it to break out of the host cell.

BIOLOGY   162

42. **Homozygous individuals...**
    (Rigorous) (Skill 5.1)

    A. have two different alleles.
    B. are of the same species.
    C. have the same features.
    D. have a pair of identical alleles.

D. Homozygous individuals have a pair of identical alleles and heterozygous individuals have two different alleles.

43. **The Law of Segregation defined by Mendel states that...**
    (Rigorous) (Skill 5.1)

    A. when sex cells form, the two alleles that determine a trait will end up on different gametes.
    B. only one of two alleles is expressed in a heterozygous organism.
    C. the allele expressed is the dominant allele.
    D. alleles of one trait do not affect the inheritance of alleles on another chromosome.

A. The law of segregation states that the two alleles for each trait segregate into different gametes.

44. **When a white flower is crossed with a red flower, incomplete dominance can be seen by the production of which of the following?**
    (Average Rigor) (Skill 5.1)

    A. pink flowers
    B. red flowers
    C. white flowers
    D. red and white flowers

A. Incomplete dominance is when the F_1 generation results in an appearance somewhere between the parents. Red flowers crossed with white flowers results in an F_1 generation with pink flowers.

45.   A child with type O blood has a father with type A blood and a mother
       with type B blood. The genotypes of the parents respectively would be
       which of the following?
       (Average Rigor) (Skill 5.1)

   A. AA and BO
   B. AO and BO
   C. AA and BB
   D. AO and OO

B. Type O blood has 2 recessive O genes. A child receives one allele from each
parent; therefore, each parent in this example must have an O allele. The father has
type A blood with a genotype of AO and the mother has type B blood with a genotype of
BO.

46.   All the following statements regarding both a mitochondria and a
       chloroplast are correct except...
       (Rigorous) (Skill 5.3)

   A. they both produce energy over a gradient.
   B. they both have DNA and are capable of reproduction.
   C. they both transform light energy to chemical energy.
   D. they both make ATP.

C. Cellular respiration does not transform light energy to chemical energy. Cellular
respiration transfers electrons to release energy. Photosynthesis utilizes light energy to
produce chemical energy.

47.   Crossing over, which increases genetic diversity occurs during which
       stage(s)?
       (Average Rigor) (Skill 5.3)

   A. telophase II in meiosis
   B. metaphase in mitosis
   C. interphase in both mitosis and meiosis
   D. prophase I in meiosis

D. During prophase I of meiosis, the replicated chromosomes condense and pair with
their homologues in a process called synapsis. Crossing over, the exchange of genetic
material between homologues to further increase diversity, occurs during prophase I.

48. **Which of the following is not posttranscriptional processing?**
(Rigorous) (Skill 6.2)

A. 5' capping
B. intron splicing
C. polypeptide splicing
D. 3' polyadenylation

C. The removal of segments of polypeptides is a posttranslational process. The other three are methods of posttranscriptional processing.

49. **What is the correct order of steps in protein synthesis?**
(Easy) (Skill 6.2)

A. transcription, then replication
B. transcription, then translation
C. translation, then transcription
D. replication, then translation

B. A DNA strand first undergoes transcription to get a complementary mRNA strand. Translation of the mRNA strand then occurs to result in the tRNA adding the appropriate amino acid for an end product, a protein.

50. **This carries amino acids to the ribosome in protein synthesis.**
(Easy) (Skill 6.2)

A. messenger RNA
B. ribosomal RNA
C. transfer RNA
D. DNA

C. The tRNA molecule is specific for a particular amino acid. The tRNA has an anticodon sequence that is complementary to the codon. This specifies where the tRNA places the amino acid in protein synthesis.

51.   A DNA molecule has the sequence of ACTATG. What is the anticodon
       of this molecule?
       (Easy) (Skill 6.2)

    A. UGAUAC
    B. ACUAUG
    C. TGATAC
    D. ACTATG

B. The DNA is first transcribed into mRNA. Here, the DNA has the sequence
ACTATG; therefore, the complementary mRNA sequence is UGAUAC (remember, in
RNA, T is U). This mRNA sequence is the codon. The anticodon is the complement to
the codon. The anticodon sequence will be ACUAUG (remember, the anticodon is
tRNA, so U is present instead of T).

52.   DNA synthesis results in a strand that is synthesized continuously.
       This is the...
       (Average Rigor) (Skill 6.2)

    A. lagging strand.
    B. leading strand.
    C. template strand.
    D. complementary strand.

B. As DNA synthesis proceeds along the replication fork, one strand is replicated
continuously (the leading strand) and the other strand is replicated discontinuously (the
lagging strand).

53.   Evolution occurs in...
       (Average Rigor) (Skill 6.4)

    A. individuals.
    B. populations.
    C. organ systems.
    D. cells.

B. Evolution is a change in genotype over time. Gene frequencies shift and change
from generation to generation. Populations evolve, not individuals.

54. **Which type of cell would contain the most mitochondria?**
    (Rigorous) (Skill 6.5)

    A. muscle cell
    B. nerve cell
    C. epithelium
    D. blood cell

A. Mitochondria are the site of cellular respiration where ATP is made. Muscle cells have the most mitochondria because they use a great deal of energy.

55. **The polymerase chain reaction...**
    (Rigorous) (Skill 6.6)

    A. is a group of polymerases.
    B. is a technique for amplifying DNA.
    C. is a primer for DNA synthesis.
    D. is synthesis of polymerase.

B. PCR is a technique in which a piece of DNA can be amplified into billions of copies within a few hours.

56. **Any change that affects the sequence of bases in a gene is called a(n)...**
    (Average Rigor) (Skill 6.6)

    A. deletion.
    B. polyploid.
    C. mutation.
    D. duplication.

C. A mutation is an inheritable change in DNA. It may be an error in replication or a spontaneous rearrangement of one ore more segments of DNA. Deletion and duplication are types of mutations. Polyploidy is when and organism has more than two complete chromosome sets.

57. **Which of the following is not true regarding restriction enzymes?**
(Rigorous) (Skill 6.6)

   A. they do not aid in recombination procedures
   B. they are used in genetic engineering
   C. they are named after the bacteria in which they naturally occur
   D. they identify and splice certain base sequences on DNA

A. A restriction enzyme is a bacterial enzyme that cuts foreign DNA at specific locations. The splicing of restriction fragments into a plasmid results in a recombinant plasmid.

58. **A genetic engineering advancement in the medical field is...**
(Easy) (Skill 6.7)

   A. gene therapy.
   B. pesticides.
   C. degradation of harmful chemicals.
   D. antibiotics.

A. Gene therapy is the introduction of a normal allele to the somatic cells to replace a defective allele. The medical field has had success in treating patients with a single enzyme deficiency disease. Gene therapy has allowed doctors and scientists to introduce a normal allele that provides the missing enzyme.

59. **Given the choice of lab activities, which would you omit?**
(Easy) (Skill 6.8)

   A. a genetics experiment tracking the fur color of mice
   B. dissecting a preserved fetal pig
   C. a lab relating temperature to respiration rate using live goldfish
   D. pithing a frog to see the action of circulation

D. The use of live vertebrate organisms in a way that may harm the animal is prohibited. The observation of fur color in mice is not harmful to the animal and the use of live goldfish is acceptable because they are invertebrates. The dissection of a fetal pig is acceptable if it comes from a known origin.

60.   **Man's scientific name is Homo sapiens. Choose the proper classification beginning with kingdom and ending with order.**
        (Average Rigor) (Skill 7.1)

   A. Animalia, Vertebrata, Mammalia, Primate, Hominidae
   B. Animalia, Vertebrata, Chordata, Mammalia, Primate
   C. Animalia, Chordata, Vertebrata, Mammalia, Primate
   D. Chordata, Vertebrata, Primate, Homo, sapiens

C. The order of classification for humans is as follows: Kingdom, Animalia; Phylum, Chordata; Subphylum, Vertebrata; Class, Mammalia; Order, Primate; Family, Hominadae; Genus, Homo; Species, sapiens.

61.   **The scientific name *Canis familiaris* refers to the animal's...**
        (Average Rigor) (Skill 7.1)

   A. kingdom and phylum names.
   B. genus and species names.
   C. class and species names.
   D. order and family names.

B. Each species is scientifically known by a two-part name, or binomial. The first word in the name is the genus and the second word is its specific epithet (species name).

62.   **Members of the same species...**
        (Average Rigor) (Skill 7.1)

   A. look identical.
   B. never change.
   C. reproduce successfully within their group.
   D. live in the same geographic location.

C. Species are defined by the ability to successfully reproduce with members of their own kind.

63.   **Which phylum accounts for 85% of all animal species?**
        (Average Rigor) (Skill 7.1)

   A. Nematoda
   B. Chordata
   C. Arthropoda
   D. Cnidaria

C. The arthropoda phylum consists of insects, crustaceans, and spiders. They are the largest group in the animal kingdom.

64. **The wing of a bird, human arm, and whale flipper have the same bone structure. These are called...**
    (Average Rigor) (Skill 7.1)

    A. polymorphic structures.
    B. homologous structures.
    C. vestigial structures.
    D. analogous structures.

B. Homologous structures have the same genetic basis (leading to similar appearances), but are used for different functions.

65. **Which kingdom is comprised of organisms made of one cell with no nuclear membrane?**
    (Rigorous) (Skill 7.3)

    A. Monera
    B. Protista
    C. Fungi
    D. Algae

A. Monera is the only kingdom that is made up of unicellular organisms with no nucleus. Algae is a protist because it is made up of one type of tissue and it has a nucleus.

66. **All of the following are examples of a member of Kingdom Fungi except...**
    (Average Rigor) (Skill 7.3)

    A. mold.
    B. algae.
    C. mildew.
    D. mushrooms.

B. Mold, mildew, and mushrooms are all fungi. Brown algae and golden algae are members of the kingdom protista and green algae are members of the plant kingdom.

67. **The two major ways to determine taxonomic classification are...**
    (Rigorous) (Skill 7.4)

    A. evolution and phylogeny.
    B. reproductive success and evolution.
    C. phylogeny and morphology.
    D. size and color.

C. Taxonomy is based on structure (morphology) and evolutionary relationships (phylogeny).

68. **The term "phenotype" refers to which of the following?**
    (Easy) (Skill 8.3)

    A. a condition which is heterozygous
    B. the genetic makeup of an individual
    C. a condition which is homozygous
    D. how the genotype is expressed

D. Phenotype is the physical appearance of an organism due to its genetic makeup (genotype).

69. **The biological species concept applies to...**
    (Easy) (Skill 8.5)

    A. asexual organisms.
    B. extinct organisms.
    C. sexual organisms.
    D. fossil organisms.

C. The biological species concept states that a species is a reproductive community of populations that occupy a specific niche in nature. It focuses on reproductive isolation of populations as the primary criterion for recognition of species status. The biological species concept does not apply to organisms that are completely asexual in their reproduction, fossil organisms, or distinctive populations that hybridize.

70. **Spores are the reproduction mode for which of the following group of plants?**
(Rigorous) (Skill 9.1)

A. algae
B. flowering plants
C. conifers
D. ferns

D. Ferns are non-seeded vascular plants. All plants in this group have spores and require water for reproduction. Algae, flowering plants, and conifers are not in this group of plants.

71. **Which is the correct sequence of embryonic development in a frog?**
(Average Rigor) (Skill 9.2)

A. cleavage – blastula – gastrula
B. cleavage – gastrula – blastula
C. blastula – cleavage – gastrula
D. gastrula – blastula – cleavage

A. Animals go through several stages of development after fertilization of the egg cell. The first step is cleavage which continues until the egg becomes a blastula. The blastula is a hollow ball of undifferentiated cells. Gastrulation is the next step. This is the time of tissue differentiation into the separate germ layers: the endoderm, mesoderm, and ectoderm.

72. **Which of the following is the correct order of the stages of plant development from egg to adult plant?**
(Rigorous) (Skill 9.4)

A. morphogenesis, growth, and
   cellular differentiation
B. cell differentiation, growth, and
   morphogenesis
C. growth, morphogenesis, and
   cellular differentiation
D. growth, cellular differentiation,
   and morphogensis

C. The development of the egg to form a plant occurs in three stages: growth; morphogenesis, the development of form; and cellular differentiation, the acquisition of a cell's specific structure and function.

73. **The process in which pollen grains are released from the anthers is called...**
(Easy) (Skill 9.4)

    A. pollination.
    B. fertilization.
    C. blooming.
    D. dispersal.

A. Pollen grains are released from the anthers during pollination and carried by animals and the wind to land on the carpels.

74. **Which of the following is not a characteristic of a monocot?**
(Rigorous) (Skill 9.4)

    A. parallel veins in leaves
    B. petals of flowers occur in multiples of 4 or 5
    C. one seed leaf
    D. vascular tissue scattered throughout the stem

B. Monocots have one cotelydon, parallel veins in their leaves, and their flower petals are in multiples of threes. Dicots have flower petals in multiples of fours and fives.

75. **How are angiosperms different from other groups of plants?**
(Average Rigor) (Skill 9.4)

    A. presence of flowers and fruits
    B. production of spores for reproduction
    C. true roots and stems
    D. seed production

A. Angiosperms do not have spores for reproduction. They do have true roots and stems, as do all vascular plants. They do have seed production, as do the gymnosperms. The presence of flowers and fruits is the difference between angiosperms and other plants.

76. **Generations of plants alternate between...**
(Rigorous) (Skill 9.4)

    A. angiosperms and bryophytes.
    B. flowering and nonflowering stages.
    C. seed bearing and spore bearing plants.
    D. haploid and diploid stages.

D. Reproduction of plants is accomplished through alteration of generations. Simply stated, a haploid stage in the plant's life history alternates with a diploid stage.

77. **Double fertilization refers to which of the following?**
    (Average Rigor) (Skill 9.4)

    A. two sperm fertilizing one egg
    B. fertilization of a plant by gametes from two separate plants
    C. two sperm enter the plant embryo sac; one sperm fertilizes the egg, the other forms the endosperm
    D. the production of non-identical twins through fertilization of two separate eggs

C. In angiosperms, double fertilization is when an ovum is fertilized by two sperm. One sperm produces the new plant and the other forms the food supply for the developing plant (endosperm).

78. **What is necessary for diffusion to occur?**
    (Average Rigor) (Skill 10.1)

    A. carrier proteins
    B. energy
    C. a concentration gradient
    D. a membrane

C. Diffusion is the ability of molecules to move from areas of high concentration to areas of low concentration (a concentration gradient).

79. **As the amount of waste production increases in a cell, the rate of excretion...**
    (Rigorous) (Skill 10.1)

    A. slowly decreases.
    B. remains the same.
    C. increases.
    D. stops due to cell death.

C. Homeostasis is the control of the differences between internal and external environments. Excretion is the homeostatic system that regulates the amount of waste in a cell. As the amount of waste increases, the rate of excretion will increase to maintain homeostasis.

80. **Identify the correct sequence of organization of living things.**
    (Rigorous) (Skill 10.2)

    A. cell – organelle – organ system – tissue – organ – organism
    B. cell – tissue – organ – organ system – organelle – organism
    C. organelle – cell – tissue – organ – organ system – organism
    D. tissue – organelle – organ – cell – organism – organ system

C. An organism, such as a human, is comprised of several organ systems such as the circulatory and nervous systems. These organ systems consist of many organs including the heart and the brain. These organs are made of tissue such as cardiac muscle. Tissues are made up of cells, which contain organelles like the mitochondria and the Golgi apparatus.

81. **Which is not a characteristic of living things?**
    (Rigorous) (Skill 10.3)

    A. movement
    B. cellular structure
    C. metabolism
    D. reproduction

A. Movement is not a characteristic of life. Viruses are considered non-living organisms but have the ability to move from cell to cell in its host organism.

82. **Which is the correct statement regarding the human nervous system and the human endocrine system?**
    (Average Rigor) (Skill 10.3)

    A. the nervous system maintains homeostasis whereas the endocrine system does not
    B. endocrine glands produce neurotransmitters whereas nerves produce hormones
    C. nerve signals travel on neurons whereas hormones travel through the blood
    D. the nervous system involves chemical transmission whereas the endocrine system does not

C. In the human nervous system, neurons carry nerve signals to and from the cell body. Endocrine glands produce hormones that are carried through the body in the bloodstream.

83.   In angiosperms, the food for the developing plant is found in which of the following structures?
(Rigorous) (Skill 10.4)

A. ovule
B. endosperm
C. male gametophyte
D. cotyledon

B. The endosperm is a product of double fertilization. It is the food supply for the developing plant.

84.   If the niches of two species overlap, what usually results?
(Average Rigor) (Skill 10.4)

A. a symbiotic relationship
B. cooperation
C. competition
D. a new species

C. Two species that occupy the same habitat or eat the same food are said to be in competition with each other.

85.   Oxygen created in photosynthesis comes from the breakdown of...
(Easy) (Skill 10.4)

A. carbon dioxide.
B. water.
C. glucose.
D. carbon monoxide.

B. In photosynthesis, water is split; the hydrogen atoms are pulled to carbon dioxide which is taken in by the plant and ultimately reduced to make glucose. The oxygen from the water is given off as a waste product.

86.   The first cells that evolved on earth were probably of which type?
(Rigorous) (Skill 11.1)

A. autotrophs
B. eukaryotes
C. heterotrophs
D. prokaryotes

D. Prokaryotes date back to 3.5 billion years ago in the first fossil record. Their ability to adapt to the environment allows them to thrive in a wide variety of habitats.

87. **What controls gas exchange on the bottom of a plant leaf?**
    (Average Rigor) (Skill 11.3)

    A. stomata
    B. epidermis
    C. collenchyma and schlerenchyma
    D. palisade mesophyll

A. Stomata provide openings on the underside of leaves for oxygen to move in or out of the plant and for carbon dioxide to move in.

88. **All of the following are found in the dermis layer of skin except...**
    (Easy) (Skill 11.3)

    A. sweat glands.
    B. keratin.
    C. hair follicles.
    D. blood vessels.

B. Keratin is a water proofing protein found in the epidermis.

89. **The role of neurotransmitters in nerve action is...**
    (Easy) (Skill 12.1)

    A. to turn off the sodium pump.
    B. to turn off the calcium pump.
    C. to send impulses to neurons.
    D. to send impulses to the body.

A. The neurotransmitters turn off the sodium pump, which results in depolarization of the membrane.

90. **Fats are broken down by which substance?**
    (Rigorous) (Skill 12.1)

    A. bile produced in the gall bladder
    B. lipase produced in the gall bladder
    C. glucagons produced in the liver
    D. bile produced in the liver

D. The liver produces bile, which breaks down and emulsifies fatty acids.

91. **Fertilization in humans usually occurs in the...**
    (Easy) (Skill 12.1)

    A. uterus.
    B. ovary.
    C. fallopian tubes.
    D. vagina.

C. Fertilization of the egg by the sperm normally occurs in the fallopian tube. The fertilized egg is then implanted on the uterine lining for development.

92. **Food is carried through the digestive tract by a series of wave-like contractions. This process is called...**
    (Easy) (Skill 12.1)

    A. peristalsis.
    B. chyme.
    C. digestion.
    D. absorption.

A. Peristalsis is the process of wave-like contractions that moves food through the digestive tract.

93. **Movement is possible by the action of muscles pulling on...**
    (Easy) (Skill 12.1)

    A. skin.
    B. bones.
    C. joints.
    D. ligaments.

B. The muscular system's function is for movement. Skeletal muscles are attached to bones and are responsible for their movement.

94. **All of the following are functions of the skin except...**
    (Easy) (Skill 12.1)

    A. storage.
    B. protection.
    C. sensation.
    D. regulation of temperature.

A. Skin is a protective barrier against infection. It contains hair follicles that respond to sensation and it plays a role in thermoregulation.

95.   **A school age boy had the chicken pox as a baby. He will most likely not get this disease again because of...**
(Average Rigor) (Skill 12.1)

A. passive immunity.
B. vaccination.
C. antibiotics.
D. active immunity.

D. Active immunity develops after recovery from an infectious disease, such as the chicken pox, or after vaccination. Passive immunity may be passed from one individual to another (from mother to nursing child).

96.   **Hormones are essential to the regulation of reproduction. What organ is responsible for the release of hormones for sexual maturity?**
(Average) (Skill 12.2)

A. pituitary gland
B. hypothalamus
C. pancreas
D. thyroid gland

B. The hypothalamus begins secreting hormones that help mature the reproductive system and stimulate development of the secondary sex characteristics.

97.   **All of the following are density independent factors that affect a population except...**
(Average Rigor) (Skill 13.5)

A. temperature.
B. rainfall.
C. predation.
D. soil nutrients.

C. As a population increases, the competition for resources is intense and the growth rate declines. This is a density-dependent factor. An example of this would be predation. Density-independent factors affect the population regardless of its size. Examples of density-independent factors are rainfall, temperature, and soil nutrients.

98.   A clownfish is protected by the sea anemone's tentacles. In turn, the anemone receives uneaten food from the clownfish. This is an example of...
      (Easy) (Skill 13.5)

      A. mutualism.
      B. parasitism.
      C. commensalisms.
      D. competition.

A. Neither the clownfish nor the anemone cause harmful effects towards one another and they both benefit from their relationship. Mutualism is when two species that occupy a similar space benefit from their relationship.

99.   **High humidity and temperature stability are present in which of the following biomes?**
      (Average Rigor) (Skill 14.1)

      A. taiga
      B. deciduous forest
      C. desert
      D. tropical rain forest

D. A tropical rain forest is located near the equator. Its temperature is at a constant 25 degrees C and the humidity is high due to the rainfall that exceeds 200 cm per year.

100. **Which of the following is not an abiotic factor?**
      (Rigorous) (Skill 14.1)

      A. temperature
      B. rainfall
      C. soil quality
      D. bacteria

D. Abiotic factors are non-living aspects of an ecosystem. Bacteria is an example of a biotic factor—a living thing.

101. **If DDT were present in an ecosystem, which of the following   organisms would have the highest concentration in its system?**
(Average Rigor) (Skill 14.3)

A. grasshopper
B. eagle
C. frog
D. crabgrass

B. Chemicals and pesticides accumulate along the food chain. Tertiary consumers have more accumulated toxins than animals at the bottom of the food chain.

102. **Which trophic level has the highest ecological efficiency?**
(Rigorous) (Skill 15.1)

A. decomposers
B. producers
C. tertiary consumers
D. secondary consumers

B. The amount of energy that is transferred between trophic levels is called the ecological efficiency. The visual of this is represented in a pyramid of productivity. The producers have the greatest amount of energy and are at the bottom of this pyramid.

103. **Primary succession occurs after...**
(Rigorous) (Skill 15.5)

A. nutrient enrichment.
B. a forest fire.
C. bare rock is exposed after a water table recedes.
D. a housing development is built.

C. Primary succession occurs where life never existed before, such as flooded areas or a new volcanic island. It is only after the water recedes that the rock is able to support new life.

104. **A student designed a science project testing the effects of light and water on plant growth. You would recommend that she...**
(Rigorous) (Skill 16.1)

    A. manipulate the temperature as well.
    B. also alter the pH of the water as another variable.
    C. omit either water or light as a variable.
    D. also alter the light concentration as another variable.

C. In science, experiments should be designed so that only one variable is manipulated at a time.

105. **Which biome is the most prevalent on Earth?**
(Easy) (Skill 14.1)

    A. marine
    B. desert
    C. savanna
    D. tundra

A. The marine biome covers 75% of the Earth. This biome is organized by the depth of water.

106. **A scientific theory...**
(Average Rigor) (Skill 16.2)

    A. proves scientific accuracy.
    B. is never rejected.
    C. results in a medical breakthrough.
    D. may be altered at a later time.

D. Scientific theory is usually accepted and verified information but can always be changed at anytime.

107. **Which is the correct order of methodology? 1) testing a revised explanation, 2) setting up a controlled experiment to test an explanation, 3) drawing a conclusion, 4) suggesting an explanation for observations, and 5) comparing observed results to hypothesized results**
(Average Rigor) (Skill 16.3)

A. 4, 2, 3, 1, 5
B. 3, 1, 4, 2, 5
C. 4, 2, 5, 1, 3
D. 2, 5, 4, 1, 3

C. The first step in scientific inquiry is posing a question to be answered. Next, a hypothesis is formed to provide a plausible explanation. An experiment is then proposed and performed to test this hypothesis. A comparison between the predicted and observed results is the next step. Conclusions are then formed and it is determined whether the hypothesis is correct or incorrect. If incorrect, the next step is to form a new hypothesis and repeat the process.

108. **Identify the control in the following experiment. A student grew four plants under the following conditions and was measuring photosynthetic rate by measuring mass. 2 plants in 50% light and 2 plants in 100% light.**
(Average Rigor) (Skill 16.5)

A. plants grown with no added nutrients
B. plants grown in the dark
C plants in 100% light
D. plants in 50% light

C. The 100% light plants are those that the student will be comparing the 50% plants to. This will be the control.

109. **In an experiment measuring the growth of bacteria at different temperatures, identify the independent variable.**
(Average Rigor) *(Skill 16.5)*

A. growth of number of colonies
B. temperature
C. type of bacteria used
D. light intensity

B. The independent variable is controlled by the experimenter. Here, the temperature is controlled to determine its effect on the growth of bacteria (dependent variable).

110. Biological waste should be disposed of...
(Easy) (Skill 17.1)

A. in the trash can.
B. under a fume hood.
C. in the broken glass box.
D. in an autoclavable biohazard bag.

D. Biological material should never be stored near food or water used for human consumption. All biological material should be appropriately labeled. All blood and body fluids should be put in a well-contained container with a secure lid to prevent leaking. All biological waste should be disposed of in biological hazardous waste bags.

111. Chemicals should be stored...
(Easy) (Skill 17.1)

A. in a cool dark room.
B. in a dark room.
C. according to their reactivity with other substances.
D. in a double locked room.

C. All chemicals should be stored with other chemicals of similar reactivity. Failure to do so could result in an undesirable chemical reaction.

112. The "Right to Know" law states...
(Rigorous) (Skill 17.1)

A. the inventory of toxic chemicals checked against the "Substance List" be available.
B. that students are to be informed of alternatives to dissection.
C. that science teachers are to be informed of student allergies.
D. that students are to be informed of infectious microorganisms used in lab.

A. The right to know law pertains to chemical substances in the lab. Employees should check the material safety data sheets and the substance list for potential hazards in the lab.

113. **A light microscope has an ocular of 10X and an objective of 40X. What is the total magnification?**
    (Easy) (Skill 17.1)

    A. 400X
    B. 30X
    C. 50X
    D. 4000X

A. To determine the total magnification of a microscope, multiply the ocular lens by the objective lens. Here, the ocular lens is 10X and the objective lens is 40X.

   (10X) X (40X) = 400X total magnification

114. **Electrophoresis separates DNA on the basis of...**
    (Rigorous) (Skill 17.1)

    A. amount of current.
    B. molecular size.
    C. positive charge of the molecule.
    D. solubility of the gel.

B. Electrophoresis uses electrical charges of molecules to separate them according to their size.

115. **Which is not a correct statement regarding the use of a light microscope?**
    (Easy) (Skill 17.1)

    A. carry the microscope with two hands
    B. store on the low power objective
    C. clean all lenses with lens paper
    D. focus first on high power

D. Always begin focusing on low power. This allows for the observation of microorganisms in a larger field of view. Switch to high power once you have a microorganism in view on low power.

116. **Spectrophotometry utilizes the principle of...**
(Easy) (Skill 17.1)

A. light transmission.
B. molecular weight.
C. solubility of the substance.
D. electrical charges.

A. Spectrophotometry uses percent of light at different wavelengths absorbed and transmitted by a pigment solution.

117. **Chromotography is most often associated with the separation of...**
(Average) (Skill 17.1)

A. nutritional elements.
B. DNA.
C. proteins.
D. plant pigments.

D. Chromatography uses the principles of capillarity to separate substances such as plant pigments. Molecules of a larger size will move slower up the paper, whereas smaller molecules will move more quickly producing lines of pigment.

118. **The reading of a meniscus in a graduated cylinder is done at the...**
(Easy) (Skill 17.1)

A. top of the meniscus.
B. middle of the meniscus.
C. bottom of the meniscus.
D. closest whole number.

C. The graduated cylinder is the common instrument used for measuring volume. It is important for the accuracy of the measurement to read the volume level of the liquid at the bottom of the meniscus. The meniscus is the curved surface of the liquid.

XAMonline, INC. 21 Orient Ave. Melrose, MA 02176
Toll Free number 800-509-4128
TO ORDER Fax 781-662-9268 OR www.XAMonline.com
GEORGIA ASSESSMENTS FOR THE CERTIFICATION OF
EDUCATORS   -GACE - 2008

P0#   Store/School:

Address 1:

Address 2 (Ship to other):

City, State Zip

Credit card number_____-_____-_____-_____   expiration_____
EMAIL _____
PHONE   **FAX**

13# ISBN 2007	TITLE	Qty	Retail	Total
978-1-58197-257-3	Basic Skills 200, 201, 202			
978-1-58197-528-4	Biology 026, 027			
978-1-58197-584-0	Science 024, 025			
978-1-58197-341-9	English 020, 021			
978-1-58197-569-7	Physics 030, 031			
978-1-58197-531-4	Art Education Sample Test 109, 110			
978-1-58197-545-1	History 034, 035			
978-1-58197-774-5	Health and Physical Education 115, 116			
978-1-58197-540-6	Chemistry 028, 029			
978-1-58197-534-5	Reading 117, 118			
978-1-58197-547-5	Media Specialist 101, 102			
978-1-58197-535-2	Middle Grades Reading 012			
978-1-58197-591-8	Middle Grades Science 014			
978-1-58197-345-7	Middle Grades Mathematics 013			
978-1-58197-686-1	Middle Grades Social Science 015			
978-158-197-598-7	Middle Grades Language Arts 011			
978-1-58197-346-4	Mathematics 022, 023			
978-1-58197-549-9	Political Science 032, 033			
978-1-58197-588-8	Paraprofessional Assessment 177			
978-1-58197-589-5	Professional Pedagogy Assessment 171, 172			
978-1-58197-259-7	Early Childhood Education 001, 002			
978-1-58197-587-1	School Counseling 103, 104			
978-1-58197-541-3	Spanish 141, 142			
978-1-58197-610-6	Special Education General Curriculum 081, 082			
978-1-58197-530-7	French Sample Test 143, 144			
			SUBTOTAL	
	FOR PRODUCT PRICES GO TO WWW.XAMONLINE.COM		Ship	$8.25
			TOTAL	

119. **Which item should always be used when using chemicals with noxious vapors?**
(Easy) (Skill 17.3)

A. eye protection
B. face shield
C. fume hood
D. lab apron

C. Fume hoods are designed to protect the experimenter from chemical fumes. The three other choices do not prevent chemical fumes from entering the respiratory system.

120. **Who should be notified in the case of a serious chemical spill?**
(Easy)(Skill 17.4)

I. the custodian
II. the fire department
III. the chemistry teacher
IV. the administration

A. I
B. II
C. II and III
D. II and IV

D. For large spills, the school administration and the local fire department should be notified.

121. **In which situation would a science teacher be liable?**
(Average Rigor) (Skill 17.4)

A. a teacher leaves to receive an emergency phone call and a student slips and falls
B. a student removes their goggles and gets dissection fluid in their eye
C. a faulty gas line results in a fire
D. a students cuts themselves with a scalpel

A. A teacher has an obligation to be present in the lab at all times. If the teacher needs to leave, an appropriate substitute is needed.

122. Which statement best defines negligence?
(Average Rigor) (Skill 17.4)

A. failure to give oral instructions for those with reading disabilities
B. failure to exercise ordinary care
C. inability to supervise a large group of students
D. reasonable anticipation that an event may occur

B. Negligence is the failure to exercise ordinary or reasonable care.